ADJUSTMENT DISORDER

'lease re
this la

r

ADJUSTMENT
DISORDER

A Collection of Maladjusted Essays

PATRICK MONDACA

BAUHAN PUBLISHING
PETERBOROUGH, NEW HAMPSHIRE
2021

Library of Congress Cataloging-in-Publication Data

Names: Mondaca, Patrick, author.
Title: Adjustment disorder : a collection of maladjusted essays / Patrick Mondaca.
Description: Peterborough, New Hampshire : Bauhan Publishing, [2021] | Includes
bibliographical references.
Identifiers: LCCN 2021006939 (print) | LCCN 2021006940 (ebook) | ISBN
9780872333277 (paperback) | ISBN 9780872333284 (ebook)
Subjects: LCSH: Mondaca, Patrick. | Adjustment disorders. | Stress (Psychology)--
Social aspects. | Adjustment disorders--Treatment. | Iraq War, 2003-2011--Personal
narratives. | Iraq War, 2003-2011--Veterans--Psychology. | Iraq War,
2003-2011--Veterans--Biography. | Veterans--United States--Psychology. | East Hartford
(Conn.)--Biography.
Classification: LCC RC455.4.S87 M65 2021 (print) | LCC RC455.4.S87
(ebook) | DDC 616.85/2 [B]--dc23
LC record available at https://lccn.loc.gov/2021006939
LC ebook record available at https://lccn.loc.gov/2021006940

Book design by Sarah Bauhan
Text set in Michael Harvey's Mentor, with Strayhorn titles
Cover Design by Henry James

Patrick Mondaca can be reached through his website:
www. patrickmondaca.com

BAUHAN
PUBLISHING LLC
PO BOX 117 PETERBOROUGH NEW HAMPSHIRE 03458
603-567-4430
WWW.BAUHANPUBLISHING.COM
Follow us on Facebook and Twitter – @bauhanpub

MANUFACTURED IN THE UNITED STATES OF AMERICA

For Amy

And for those of us who have suffered from the trauma of war, not so much to our psyches, but to our souls. And for our loved ones who, too often, have borne the brunt of our disaffectedness.

Author's Note

Most of the names that appear in these essays have been changed, with the exception of some of my former colleagues in Darfur (Ibrahim, Sanusi, Hassabo, Salah, and Daud), men to who I am much indebted.

Adjustment Disorder: Occupational and social impairment due to mild or transient symptoms which decrease work efficiency and ability to perform occupational tasks only during periods of significant stress, or symptoms controlled by continuous medication: 10%.

—US Department of Veterans Affairs

Table of Contents

Avarice (Greed)

Envy

Sloth

Preface

To understand why it's so hard to come home from wars, in places like Iraq and Afghanistan, you first need to have some idea of what it was like to be there. Why it's so hard to shake it when you return home. Except only about ten percent of Americans actually do know what it is like to go to war. Now try and come to terms with that.

You also must have an idea of what, or who, you were before you left your peacetime civilian existence. That's if you can remember. War is hell, of course, so they say. But when you are young, to the young soldier, war is also a great adventure. The existential test. A rite of passage. It is adrenaline inducing. It is terror inducing. It is never-ending boredom. It is insanity. The rules are not the same. The mind is not the same. The soul is not the same.

The Department of Veterans Affairs psychologist would later say you were suffering from "Adjustment Disorder," a temporary condition, one that you would recover from once you reintegrated into postwar life.

And for some of you, such mental maladies may indeed be temporary and short term. The weight of it, of your war experience, may slough off as easily as you shed your desert uniforms and dead, sunburnt skin and military-issued kit upon landing on the nearest Coalition tarmac. You may dump it there with the weight of everything else you once staggered under. Your Kevlar helmet. Your Interceptor body armor with its eight-pound ceramic plates. Your load-bearing vest with your ammunition, field pressure dressings, and your QuikClot powder. Your 9mm pistol holster and your rifle sling. Your three-liter hydration system. Your two-day assault pack. Your tactical flashlight and your bayonet and your tactical tomahawk. Your rifle scope and your night vision goggles. Your gas mask and your nerve agent antidote injectors in case of those ever-elusive Weapons of Mass Destruction. Your letter home—just in case—tucked tight between your chest holster and your chest plate. Right down to your lowest bid combat boots. Those were the things you carried during your war. You may leave those things all in a sad, dusty heap, still reeking of cordite and Break-Free gun cleaner, still scattering that powdery sand that you can never quite rid yourself of. Or you may continue to stagger, not able to detach yourself from what lingers from the war, from what continues to fester, like some gangrenous hematoma of the psyche.

You are different now. You did not quite adjust as they said you would. When you first arrived at Landstuhl on the medevac flights from Baghdad to Kuwait to Ramstein, they asked you the standard series of questions and handed you the questionnaires to fill out about your mental health condition.

Such questionnaires screen soldiers for violent and suicidal tendencies, having just returned from one of our country's two ongoing combat theaters. But what they don't screen you for is the fraying of your moral fibers.

As one might imagine, when returning from a war, what else might a soldier feel, other than anger or aggression, and perhaps some mistrust and derision, guilt or trepidation? You blacken the affirmative ovals for many of these questions, as did many others, but no one asks you much more about it. Instead you are given prescriptions for anxiety and depression like Klonopin and Paxil and released back into the world.

And back into the world—the civilian world that is far different from the one you have just experienced at war—you do not quite reintegrate into the civilian life you had left behind. Your adjustment disorder is not, in fact, so temporary.

Instead, you pop the pills they gave you and chase those with alcohol and disconnect from your girlfriends and wives and your families and your friends and hook up with strangers in bars and call out of work and drive drunk and stoned, and you do all of the stupid, self-destructive textbook angry veteran behaviors that you know you shouldn't be doing but you cannot seem to not do.

You buy a motorcycle and you ride it too fast and too far and you let the comforting rumble drown out the noise in your head and fill the emptiness in your soul while you vaguely register the blur of headlights and metal and miles of rough pavement hurtling past just inches from your soft flesh and bones and skin and hair. And the thought that one day another motorcycle, a newer, prettier, more powerful motorcycle, will just about be the death of you will never cross your mind.

And you will run. Not in the literal, physical, Forest Gump-like way at first, but in the metaphorical self-distancing sense and later geographically-barriered space that you create far away from everyone you once knew and loved. You will break up with your partners, and push away concerned friends and siblings, and you will ignore your mother's phone calls, and blame her for your life's shortcomings and your hurt and your frustration and shift that blame on to whoever else gets in your way.

You will not look back when you do this, when you feel slighted by someone and you decide to erase them from your life and your memory, and you will put barriers up, and you will wall them off, and harden your heart and turn your face away from them like an Old Testament deity. You will not be always completely aware of your doing this while you do it. Or you won't think you are.

But you will do it again and again, some of these things, or all of these things, until one day a few years after your war, you will be in a North African desert landscape with a boy soldier who is pointing a battered AK-47 at your face, and you will see yourself staring back at you through his too old eyes. Defiant. Angry. Eyes that have seen too much too soon. Eyes with too much of an edge to them. Eyes that are windows into a bruised soul.

And you will want to take this boy in your arms and hold him, and tell him to put the rifle down, and feel how much lighter his hands are now without it, and release him from the weight of it, and watch the light come back into his eyes, and show him your lensatic compass, and how one can find their way with it again after being lost. But you do not, and the boy doesn't want to lower his rifle away from your face, or look at a compass, and you do not see the light come back to his eyes.

You will place your sunglasses and your watch and your wad of Sudanese pounds at his plastic flip-flop-clad feet, and he will motion for you to back away with his rifle, and you will walk away a few hundred dollars less valuable, and minus another of your remaining seven or so lives, and you will be grateful to not be bleeding from a 7.62 caliber hole to the face. You will say a quick thank you to the God that you have so long neglected, and you will swear to return home and to go to church again and to not be a philandering asshole and to be a good father and to walk your dogs for as long as they want.

But you will not do any of these things. You will buy more sunglasses and more watches, and you will place those at other boys' feet with other battered rifles pointed at your face. You will say more meaningless prayers and make more insincere promises and wish that those boys will bare their bruised souls and that the edge will fade from their faces and the hate from their eyes, but it will not. And they will not. They will only fade back into the scrub, where they will wait for the next you to happen along to hold up at gunpoint.

And you will go back home. You will forget all about those boys and your prayers and your promises. You will go back to lusting after other men's wives. You will want more and more, and when you get it you will still want for more. You will drown your sorrows in booze and the days and nights will blur by like you're watching them from the inside of a too-fast-moving train. You will be a semifunctioning alcoholic and become distant and pull away from those you know and love. You will fill the void that you feel with hate and with envy and with contempt and with anger.

And on some days when you are alone, and when you are inebriated and morose and thinking about all those other soldiers who made it home from the wars only to die from cancer or suicide or substance abuse, you will wonder if you are all cursed now having been to war. You will wonder if your souls are too damaged now and if there is any coming back from the things you have done and the places you have been. You will relive those childhood sweltering summer revival meetings at the Baptist church when the evangelists would summon down fire and brimstone on all of you sinners. You will deliberate whether you are going to hell or if you are already in it.

And then one bright and sunny summer afternoon in quiet Montclair, New Jersey, you will get hit by a car while you're on your motorcycle and then by another car and then another. Your brain will bleed. Your lung will collapse. Your ribs will fracture. Your spleen will rupture. And when you come out of your coma and you are lying there staring at the dingy ceiling panels high on Valium or Dilaudid, you will recount all of your transgressions and the causes of your being there. And because your bruised right frontal lobe will no longer allow you to sleep at night, you will count your sins like sheep long into the lonely hours.

You will wonder if the toll of your iniquities has indeed been the death of your soul. If you have offended the Almighty one too many times and now those biblical warnings of your youth have finally come to pass. You will try and catalogue your sins and determine whether they fall within the Seven Capitals from which there is no return. To jailhouse-lawyer yourself free, perhaps. To throw one final Hail Mary pass and save yourself from the hellfire, maybe. And this book will be the tallying of these sins. This book will be your confession.

WRATH

There is a core of anger in the soul of almost every veteran, and we are justified in calling it bitterness, but the bitterness of one man is not the same thing as the bitterness of another. In one man it becomes a consuming flame that sears his soul and burns his body. In another it is barely traceable. It leads one man to outbursts of temper, another to social radicalism, a third to excesses of conservatism.

—World War I veteran Willard Waller

We Who Walk Among You

There is indeed an anger in us, those of us who have returned from one war or another. I can see this now and understand it better as the years have softened my hard edges. And I am not without a new appreciation for the relative easiness of my life in my own country, having borne witness to the abject poverty and hardships endured by those affected by war and violence in others. Yet still, I too continue to struggle with the adjustment to the peacetime life of the civilian. Too often, I find myself longing for the army life, one that seemed so absent of complication. The anger I harbor toward the complexities of civilian life, the bureaucracy, and the politics, the subtle slights, are often too much to swallow. Though, perhaps the allure of my military time may be a thing more related to a nostalgia for my younger years.

As foreign as the civilian world often seems, we devise ways of coping with our new lives. In the earliest years after my return, I buried myself in various projects and pursuits at places of employment and my universities. Others have done the same, in effort to suppress the gods of war whose voices rise up from time to time from the depths of our still fighting spirits. For those whom the call of the wanderer prevails, we run still farther to seek out the peace that alludes us. For me, I found myself back in the desert climates in Sudan, finding a serenity in my work there.

Returning home again to the urban metropolises of my own people in Philadelphia and New York City, I worked jobs as suitable to my background as could be, in police agencies and corporate investigative roles. These were with people with whom I had commonalities, some of whom had also known life under the weight or muzzle of a gun. I studied with international students with whom I shared my experience of having visited their countries, where I had gained a new respect for the ideals and liberties that so many Americans take for granted and that these students idealized. Some years later than this, I would teach my own students and answer their questions about my military experience with a newfound patience I would not have had years ago.

Thus, the following is a summary of my journey back from war and the difficulties I've encountered along the way. And while it is my experience alone, it can also be seen as a microcosm of the experiences of many others like me, who have also tried and floundered along their own road back.

In February 2003, I was a twenty-two-year-old sergeant with Connecticut's 143rd Military Police Company, deployed as a part of Operation Iraqi Freedom. Mustering out of Brainard Field, a little airstrip just south of Hartford, we were 150 soldiers, barely combat ready, even with the platoon of field-artillerymen that were volunteered by our state's military department to flesh out our ranks. The second Mother of All Battles was what it was going to be. Saddam Hussein was going to gas us. Saddam Hussein and his psychotic sons were going to rain Scud missiles down on us filled with anthrax, filled with those ever-elusive Weapons of Mass Destruction. It was going to be a street-to-street fight, in every village and every city, like in Stalingrad, like in Berlin, to the last man. At our mobilization training at Fort Drum in upstate New York, we prepared to fight in an Iraqi springtime in -14°C and six feet of snow in the dead of winter.

We did our rifle qualifications knee-deep in ice water and slush. Our rear-sight apertures glazed over and our elevation and windage knobs froze solid. Fingers were too numb to make adjustments. Targets disappeared. Bullets jammed in magazines. Bayonets stuck in sheaths. Lips turned purple against stark pale faces as bodies quivered near hypothermic shock. We huddled in warming tents and sipped tepid coffee waiting for our turn to shoot. We fired and missed and re-fired and missed some more. We re-fired and missed until we tapped out our company's ammunition allotment and had to hope for the best. We rode the old Blue Bird buses back to the barracks and took hot showers to thaw out our frozen bones. We ordered Chinese food and drank beers by the case while the snowdrifts piled up against the back door. We listened to the wind whistling through the cracks in the walls and huddled under woodland poncho liners in brown polypropylene thermals. We flipped through catalogues and purchased tactical flashlights, knives, thigh-holsters, armor plates, 550 cord, and 100-mile-per-hour-tape, all the gear the army wouldn't give us that we thought we needed, that we thought might spare our precious lives.

Much of it is fragmented now. The long flight from upstate New York. The cramped shuttle bus ride from the tarmac to Camp Pennsylvania in the Kuwaiti desert. Sandstorms. Two hundred 5.56 rounds each, a post-Vietnam-era flak vest, a rifle, pistol, bayonet, and a Desert Storm era, fiberglass-bodied Humvee. The long road north to Baghdad. Basra and Nasiriya. The rotors of the Apache gunships overhead. U2's *It's a Beautiful Day* in my headphones. Occupying the grounds of Uday Hussein's palace. 72-hour watches in the guard towers. Napping under the bridges. Guarding the old prison. Patrolling the market. Lamb burgers with egg and *jibin*, a traditional Arab cheese. The Iraqi police stations. The perpetually inebriated Iraqi cops. Snipers in the water towers. "Hawaiian-shirt Fridays." Improvised explosive devises hidden under dead dogs and piles of trash. The rumble of our heavy armor in the streets. The wails of the muezzins. The begging and pleading of the Iraqi children *Mister, give me dollar. Mister, give me water. Mister, give me food.* The medevac choppers. Ramstein Air Force Base and Kaiserslautern. Walter Reed Army Medical Center. And then back home. Back to Connecticut; to suburbia; and the metropolises.

The memories fade but the feelings are still visceral. They come flooding back. The heart races and the mouth goes dry; the palms sweat and the eyes scan desperate for an exit, any exit, blue sky, fresh air, any air. In the crowds of Times Square and Chelsea Market. In the Brooklyn Battery and Lincoln and Holland tunnels. At Penn Station and in the subways. In the casinos back home in Connecticut. In the Christmas markets far away in Cologne and Bonn. Because when I'm suffocating only Baghdad is there. I am a destroyer. I am not myself.

All these years later, somehow, I always end up back in Baghdad. I used to break things. Whiskey glasses, vodka bottles, furniture, hearts. I am not proud of myself. In Paris, I rammed a Fiat into a Mercedes-Benz under the Arc de Triomphe. Like a Greek trireme. The guy blocked my lane and boxed me in so I floored it. I guess I meant to do it. I would have done it in Baghdad without a second thought. Convoy blocked? Ram it through. Simple solution. I was sorry after the fact for startling his little dog but for not much else. Blind white sheet of rage is what it was. What I was.

I try first to give people the benefit of the doubt. Not every driver is a hostile. I try to breathe through it and keep my shit together. I roll the windows down. I search different routes with my smartphone. I flip U-turns and drive in the restricted lanes and gun it through yellow lights. Sometimes that works. Usually I just end up pounding on the steering wheel and screaming at undeserving strangers and daring God to part the Red Sea before me. But God does no such thing. To the veteran, God is a fickle ally.

In terms of solving a mere traffic problem, that is apparently beyond the powers of the Almighty. Not here. Not over *there*. Not in Europe. Not in Africa. Not anywhere.

Sometimes I find myself wandering to the other side of the tracks in the early morning, after the gym, to Lackawanna Plaza, before I go back home, to the decent side of town where I live now. In years previous it was Lackawanna Terminal, a busy local railway hub moving Montclair, New Jersey's business class to their posh offices on Wall Street and Madison Avenue. Lackawanna is no longer a train station but an ugly plaza which is home to a number of third-rate retail shops and a third-rate grocery store frequented by third-rate citizens. Now it is an attraction for vagrants and drug addicts and hangers-around and petty thieves who piss in the shadows and harass and beg and disgust the proper folks hurrying past on their way to Bay Street Station, just two blocks east by the main firehouse.

I go there to get coffee from the Dunkin Donuts. I don't even like the coffee there and I have excellent coffee at home that I like to grind myself and stare at as it steeps in an expensive French press. But I go there because of the vagrants and drug addicts and hangers-around. I make a show of illegally parking my shiny black BMW in a blue-marked handicapped spot near the entrance where they like to linger, away from the rain or sun, depending on the weather. It is an arrogant display. I know that they resent my face. They hate where I come from and where I am going after I leave them. They hate everyone that I know and everything that I have. I am now with the haves and they are now with the have-nots.

I do this so that I can feel their hate. So, I can feel the sting of their glare and the disdain in their eyes. I like to feel their hate in my blood and in my heart, in my pulse and in the adrenaline that pumps through my veins and rouses my nerves and fires the synapses of my brain and resonates in the marrow of my bones and sinew and cartilage and knuckles of my arms and wrists and fists. I want them to pound out their hate into my flesh, their hate and envy and greed and mine intermingled. I want to go again to the far edge, to the lonely mountaintop, to the barren desert, to the depth of the sea, to the nomad lands, where I must gasp for air and the light begins to fade from my eyes. I go to Lackawanna Plaza with the thought that I could possibly be attacked or accosted, ambushed or threatened, maybe even with a knife or a broken bottle, or a pistol; something grievous and unforgiving, once plunged or fired into flesh, never to be retrieved.

It would be easy to conclude that I want to be punished. That I feel shame or guilt for my sins, for my crimes, for my part in the war. Well, I do not. War is the most terrifying and thrilling thing that a soldier will ever get to experience in his lifetime, if he lives through it. And if he has lived through it, he will always miss it. And I miss it. I long for the thrill of it; in all of its senseless butchery and stupidity. My hands are not the soft hands of a writer. My face is not the clean face of a banker. I still have the rough hands and scarred face of a soldier. And soldiers fight.

I never actually have gotten out of my car at Lackawanna. But I think about doing it. Sometimes I sit there for long stretches and think about doing it. Yet I do not, because I know that this part of me is a mere residual, a recurring shadow of the war still trying to consume me.

The Department of Veteran's Affairs calls the postwar behaviors that I exhibit Adjustment Disorder: "Occupational and social impairment due to mild or transient symptoms which decrease work efficiency and ability to perform occupational tasks only during periods of significant stress, or symptoms controlled by continuous medication: 10%."

Ten percent is the token minimum disability granted by the VA to those of us veterans returning home early on in the Afghanistan and Iraq wars. Veterans who could sleep soundly no longer; who had difficulties getting back into the swing of their peacetime lives; who fought too much with our wives and spoke too harshly to our children; who drank too much in local dive bars and smoked too many cigarettes with too many townies; who could still put too much of a shine on their boots and cut too close of a shave and sober up just enough to work too many hours too many days a week; who could go through the motions of mowing lawns and facilitating birthday parties and barbeques and hanging up Christmas lights and everything else the mundanity of civilian life requires.

Adjustment Disorder is the category for those who struggle and fail at our professions, and watch stupidly as our relationships, our aspirations, and lives die slow, gasping deaths. We abuse drugs, we drink heavily, we drive recklessly, we get arrested, we fight with police officers, we loathe ourselves, we reenlist, we break things, we break ourselves, we break other people, their hearts, and their trust, and their lives. Some of us do some of these things and some of us do all of these things.

A civilized society is tasked with unteaching us those lessons from savage men learned in other savage wars: the curricula on killing and on accomplishing this task with extreme prejudice and violence of action. Herein lies the struggle. The rewiring of young minds once taught to value life, to be willing to destroy it. And to value it again once the war has ended. It is not so easy a thing. The village has chosen us to do its dirty work, but the village doesn't quite know how to bring us back.

For those of us returned but still gone, for those of us still at war, who now battle only ourselves, we are ghosts who long for a world where success means just to stay alive, and failure means just to die. We must live in this new world. And we try, until we cannot.

✛

This internal struggle going on within us, it will go on undetected. I may be the quiet one sitting next to you by the exit door on the commuter train in the starched shirt and tie pretending to flip through the *New York Times*. My khakis are neatly creased and my dress boots flawlessly shined. I am polite and alert, and my hair is nattily parted to the side. My easy gaze down the aisle from time to time does not seem abnormal. My gentle but firm stance by the exit door when the train is crowded does not offend. The silent torrent of mental calculations that I am making in my head as I assess my fellow passengers does not alarm you.

My face is a shell game. My expressions rarely mean what they seem to you. What is behind each one is a preconceived determination you will never guess. While yours is an inherent reaction to your emotions, mine are contrived. Mine are situational. I stone-face vagrants and subway singers. I smile warmly and offer my seat to expectant mothers and hold doors open for seniors. I laugh at the silly antics of small children at Pret a Manger and smile at the excitement of tourists as they point and wave at Lady Liberty when crossing the Hudson by ferry.

If you think I am seeing you though, you would be wrong. I am only seeing part of you. Mostly I am looking past you. You are a live body that I have reduced to a number. All of you have a number and your number corresponds to your survivability. Your number also corresponds to your usefulness to our survivability as a group. Some of you have a higher casualty probability through no fault of your own. You are sick. Or you are pregnant. Or you are obese. You will be slow when we will need to be fast. You will panic and seize up when we will need to be on the move.

Some of you will be more useful by means of your occupation. Your hospital scrubs or security guard uniform indicate that you may be of higher value to the group than the stockbroker or the IT guy. The construction worker with the toolbox and large lunch bag also is of value. If you appear athletic and clear eyed and alert and not nose-down in your smartphone you may also be of value. You may be relied upon to carry wounded. You may also have some military or law enforcement training of your own. And this, this will increase both your own chance of survivability and that of the group's.

I know you have a name. And a story. A job, a family, a life that you live and people that love you and whom you love. I know all of these things, and I care about none of these things. If we are having a conversation about the weather this morning and the state of our political situation, we are not. While my mouth is moving and I am making the appropriate facial expressions, I am not actually there with you. My mind is far from the weather this morning. My mind does not care about what is happening or not happening in Washington.

I am focused on the men carrying backpacks and taking random pictures within the subway station. I am staring at the loose piece of luggage in the back end of the subway car. I am looking far beyond your face and obsessing over the wide sidewalks packed with tourists and New Yorkers making their way to work or school or home. I am looking at the dozens of cargo vans and SUVs driving by these sidewalks at any given time of the day. I am looking at the terraces above our heads and the rooftops and fire escapes winding up and down the sides of buildings.

But I will never tell you any of these things while I do them. You will never guess what I am thinking or the survivability number that I have assigned you. While you continue to blather on about property taxes and toll fare hikes and the quality of your cold-brewed coffees, I am no longer here with you. Instead, I am measuring sectors of fire in the four blocks ahead of me and behind me. I am calculating the distance to the nearest place of cover in the event of incoming fire or bombardment. I am calculating the amount of roadway I will need to spin my hypothetical convoy around and reroute it to safety. I am watching cars as they run over stray bags of trash on Broadway and wondering which one will get the molten-copper shaped charge through the engine block.

The man selling Italian ice from the cart outside the courthouse reminds me of the man selling ice in the market outside the airport in Baghdad. That man did not want to move his table back from the road and he angrily waived the knife he used to break chunks of ice off for customers at my team leader. I thought for a moment I might have to shoot this man. I am glad the Italian ice man does not also have a knife with him. I am glad I do not have to decide whether or not to shoot the Italian ice man before he stabs my friend. I am glad to be thirty-six now and in New York and not twenty-two in Baghdad maybe about to end a man's life who was having a shit day and who was just trying to feed his family.

These are the things I am focusing on while you prattle on about your new au pair's great pair of perky little tits and your wife's lack of interest in you and your stupid kid's anger management issues on the lacrosse team. These are the things that I am thinking about as you whine about your accrued vacation time and your lack of time to take that vacation time due to your demanding schedule and those never-ending supervisory responsibilities. The ever-increasing global demands that have you bouncing between time zones and that keep you from your personal training sessions at Equinox that you so need to destress.

You talk to me as if I am like you. Or like I care about such things as you do. But I am not you. And I do not care about those things. I think your job is shit. I think your supervisory problems are shit. I think your au pair hates you and your wife hates you both. I think your kids are sociopathic little opportunists and when you stop catering to them, they will hate you all too. That's what I think. These are the things that I am really thinking about in addition to your survivability number.

Well, if you really want to know, you probably won't make it. You're too soft. And out of shape. And lazy. And you're entitled. Where that Mexican kid who schleps the cream cheese on your bagel every morning will fight to live and push aside his fears and pull that Haitian girl who you refuse to tip thirty cents in change out of that now burning bodega, you, you will not. Your number is a three. You are a three on the ten-scale. If you survive it will be sheer luck of the draw and nothing else.

In this participation prize-type world in which we live. In this world of comb over diplomacy and social media braggadocio. In this world of shin-splint excuses and capitalist superiority and privileged this color and underprivileged that, remember that all of this bullshit existence which you cherish is only possible because of those of us who walk among you. Who walk among you unseen and who nod somberly and look far beyond your vacation hours and your au pair's tits and your wife's animosity and only measure your worth by your survivability potential.

In the end, you are just a number. And the Mexican kid that spreads the cream cheese on your bagel who you can never remember his name, his number is likely higher than yours. Do not forget this. Tip the Haitian girl her thirty fucking cents. At least you will die with a clear conscience. Try and do one good thing before they put you in the ground. Mean something to someone. To anyone. That quiet one you ramble to on the morning PATH train, to him you will mean nothing. To your wife and your kids and your au pair and your employees you will mean nothing. But mean something. At least be remembered fondly by someone.

So know this: While you are in your executive suite with the view, fantasizing about that new nineteen-year-old intern, watching YouTube videos of your future luxury yacht, or talking about those recent gains due to your aggressive CrossFit protein regimen at the local Equinox, gloating over that high-value account you just orchestrated for the firm, we are also here, we who walk among you, we who have ridden the whirlwind. We who, in the words of Oliver Wendell Holmes, *have shared the incommunicable experience of war; we have felt, we still feel, the passion of life to its top.*

Us, your lowly employees. Your Tax Credit Heroes, we look just like you in our crisp new suits and ties, crammed into our cubicle farms, put out to the proverbial civilian pasture. We report to you now instead of our sergeants and captains. We look like you now and answer to you for the moment, but we are not you. You see dollars and conquests, we see people who move about like drones, stagnant, miserable. We see false glory and pretense and lies. We see corporate bullshit about "adding value" and "books of business" and "takeaways" and we pity you. We pity you all because this is your entire life. This is the height of it, your existence. At the end of the day, you have only ever surmounted an Everest of zeroes on an Excel spreadsheet.

So, in summary, I quit. I quit this silly job. I quit this silly charade. Take my suit and tie, stuff it full of your numbers and spreadsheets, and prop it up at my desk. I guarantee that my effigy's productivity will be about the same. Or not. I won't be there to listen to your quarterly reviews anyway. And don't bother to look for me. While the most exciting part of your day is procuring your shitty mechanized coffee from the break room with the other drones, I'll be gone—sun in my face, wind at my back, path uncharted. I am a leaf in autumn, falling. I am an arrow in flight, singing. I am a free man, without regret.

The Desert

Imagine there's a point when it's just so damn hot in that gas mask, and that cool, sweet-tasting crevice of air is so close, and the pitch-black sky is so full of countless stars that after a while, when the Scud sirens start wailing, you just stop giving a shit. Instead, you remember the Patriot missile batteries you saw at the airport coming in, and the reports on CNN showing those comforting, arcing projectiles hurtling into the air at Saddam's Scuds, and you start weighing the odds in your head, betting it all on the Patriot batteries, inching that mask just a bit higher off your mouth and nose.

As the minutes tick by—ten hours left on your twelve-hour shift— you feel like you're literally melting, your skin sloughing off your bones like you've been dipped in white phosphorus. And then you remind yourself that you are just sweating so profusely within your charcoal-lined MOPP suit and gas mask that you can't tell the difference between the sweat pouring off your face and brow and the condensation fogging up your mask as your breaths grow faster and shorter and you try not to think about passing out.

So, you force yourself to think about other things, like what you will do in the event your skin starts to boil if those Patriot teams miss and one of those Scuds actually lands. You check your gas mask case strapped to your leg for the umpteenth time, feeling around in the dark with your fingers, for your Nerve Agent Antidote Kit (NAAK). You vaguely remember that *two anti-nerve agent drugs—atropine sulfate and pralidoxime chloride—each in injectable form, constitute the kit*, and that in the event of a chemical or biological attack, you will pop the caps off your auto injector pens and jam the needles through your MOPP suit bottoms and BDU trousers into your thigh. After that you're supposed to hope for the best I guess, while maintaining 360-degree security of your perimeter.

That thought kills a minute or so. By then it's so foggy inside your mask that you can't see out your lenses anyway. And you debate maybe just lifting it up over your parched, dry lips and sucking in some of that cool, delicious air and maybe stealing a quick sip of your warm, plastic-tasting water for a few more minutes. And then you do it. It's glorious and the air is just fine and smells like burnt desert and not sweet like you imagine the gas would smell like. The condensation begins to clear just enough to see a little and you hope no one is about to come over that berm and shoot at you because you know that then, without a doubt, you would be a casualty of war. Probably before you could even get a shot off.

You would die right then and there with your foggy mask on and your Vietnam War-era flak vest because Connecticut sent you to war with no body armor and then it occurs to you that you're in the National Guard for Christ's sake. You grew up in East Hartford. And now you're here in Kuwait, on the southern border of Iraq, waiting, guarding a fence against an enemy you can't see or hear or shoot if you had to, listening to Scud missile warning sirens. And so you choose. You choose to tilt that mask up over your mouth and nose and breathe in that cool, nighttime desert air. You haven't seen a Scud or Patriot fired overhead yet. Not a tracer round or aircraft or anything anywhere. Nothing but miles of endless empty desert. And you think, I might just actually live through this. Just eight more hours to go. And then only a year to go. One minute at a time.

These are the things you think about on the eve of your war. When your mettle is finally going to be tested, after nearly a month of sweating in the Kuwaiti desert. Last week the platoon went down to the port to retrieve the trucks from the motor pool. Dozens of US Army Humvees, dump trucks, ambulances, fuel trucks, and water purification vehicles were parked in long rows and awaiting their drivers. The platoon's drivers and company mechanics worked quickly in the heat to crank up stalled engines. Gunners, team leaders, and medics stalked through the motor pool, scavenging anything not nailed down that might be useful.

The motor pool is a frenzy. Units coming in, units going out. Brits, Australians, Americans, Italians, Romanians, Estonians all queuing around, stacks of parts, boxes of ammunition, water, and food rations.

Countries you didn't even know still had armies. Everyone wanted a piece of this war.

It is like the Serengeti with us stalking herds of dumb trucks. We pick them apart and scatter gear and empty containers like flesh and bones. Need a spare starter? The mechanics are in heaven. Rip one out of a brand-new truck and leave the carcass. Take everything and anything Connecticut never gave you.

Brand new portable generator? Grab one! Need a tire? Missing a door? Rip it off another and throw it in. Cannibalize it. Take it. Expropriate. Reapportion. Whatever. Anything is for the taking. Whole units of trucks and gear left behind in the dust. Brand new gear. Nothing like your old National Guard gear.

You decide that you should be doing something to prepare your station. You're the gunner, so you will do gunnerly things. You decide to grease up your turret till it glides back and forth silently and deadly without a hint of resistance. You lubricate those rusty ball bearings and pintles and joints and hinges and swivels, and rock back and forth, left turn, right turn,180 degrees, 360 degrees, you spin. You make circles in your turret. You slam it, lock it down, move it like it is 1989 and new off the lot. It occurs to you that this piece of shit was probably here for the first Gulf War. That this truck was here when you were probably nine or ten. You say welcome back then, truck. We ride again. And you continue to spin.

You make mental calculations about your spin radius. You decide you will wear everything above the waist. You will ditch your gas mask and keep it at your feet. You will strap your pistol holster to your chest. You will ditch your M16 rifle for the 12-gauge Mossberg shotgun and lay that across the turret hatch's folded cover.

You will trade your M9 bayonet to a British "sapper" for a bottle of wine because you know that you won't see wine in Baghdad, and you won't use the bayonet. The bayonet is heavy. It will weigh you down in the turret. It is bulky and you want to be light. You want to spin freely and quickly and you have two other knives, a serrated combat folder and some other sort of cool-looking dagger you bought at the PX. You don't need another knife.

You decide that war is infinitely better than stateside Guard duty.

War is practical. War makes sense. If you need something you take it. If it weighs you down, you leave it. There is an urgency and practicality and pragmatism to the wartime army that gets lost in the minefields of its peacetime bureaucracy.

You resent the National Guard now. You recount the endless counting on drill weekends of crap gear in the platoon storage areas of the Hartford Armory. Hours upon hours of cleaning already spotless weapons, reorganizing equipment in the storage connexes, mind-numbing, useless labor that never made sense to you back home. Within the confines of the Guard there was always a palatable sense of astonishing futility amongst the lower ranks. Training, training, training, and for what? You're from New England. You've spent the entirety of your enlistment wandering about the leafy woods and fertile loam of the Connecticut River Valley and very much not preparing for war in a fucking sandy desert.

You're from a lower-class family and you joined at seventeen for the college money, all a bit of a blur. Now you're twenty-two and you're in the middle of a desert going to fight in the Mother of All Wars against Saddam's legions. Road marching in four feet of snow in upstate New York to prepare for a war in the Middle East made no sense to you. Firing rifles at forest green plastic Ivans, knocking icicles off your front and rear sight apertures in -14°C, and learning how to treat cold-weather casualties made no sense to you. But this, this war in the desert, this makes perfect sense.

Now things are clear. You have heard about the rapes and the torture and the killings and the poison gas and the crimes against humanity perpetrated by the Hussein regime and it angers you. You are happy to be part of this war now. There is a sense of embarking on the "great crusade" of your own generation, one of justice and peace and vengeance for what the Iraqi people have suffered at the hands of Saddam Hussein and his sons. You feel for them. This is the thing you tell yourself as you feel yourself perspiring in the early morning sun. This is the thing you tell yourself when you look at those active-army guys with their body armor and you look at your post-Vietnam War era flak vest. You will make do as others have before you in worse places.

You take comfort in the fact that you have brought your department-issued body armor from home where you are a police officer and you will wear this under your shitty National Guard-issued vest. You are a smart gunner. A specialist gunner who has learned a few things and seen some things. You gave back your corporal stripes when you came back from Italy at last year's annual training. You didn't want to lead a team, you said. You were happy on the gun, you said. And you were. Still, sitting in your fiberglass-skinned piece of shit with sandbags packed around the turret, you look at those active-army MPs with their up-armored vehicles and you envy them and resent the Guard some more.

You decide that fighting a war in a fucking desert will be infinitely better than fighting a war in the woods. In the desert there are no extravagancies. There is an absence of fluff. The desert warfighter is stripped down. A bareknuckle fighter. A desert army must adapt or die. And out of such necessity emerges a practicality and good sense that you have never before experienced back at home.

But problems remain. The Mk 19 grenade launcher that you have devoted hours learning to clean, fire, and disassemble will be of no use in the urban battlespace you are about to occupy. The Mk 19's 40mm round will take eighteen to thirty meters to arm once it is fired, which is utterly useless to you in most law-and-order operations. Eighteen to thirty meters translates to roughly sixty to one hundred feet. In Baghdad, you will be conducting tactical overwatch for military police teams performing crowd control and foot patrols in crowded marketplaces. At those ranges an Mk 19 would be a dead weight—all 99.6 glorious pounds of sheer teeth-chattering, soul-shaking American-forged death and steel. A mere human paper punch boring holes in flesh and steel and scattering high explosive well past its targets. Seems like someone should have thought of this dilemma long before deploying to Baghdad. The National Guard. Or the armorers at least. Or you for Christ's sake. After all, you're the fucking gunner. This is your livelihood, your bread and butter. You are the guardian angel for your team.

Instead you mount your driver's M249, a light machine gun with which you are vaguely familiar. Now you will be stuck with this sand magnet of a weapon, fine desert powder lining every oily crevice and opening of its delicate ammunition feed and short barrel. You are insulted by this weapon, and you say a silent prayer to the gods of war that it will fire when you pull that trigger. You will be a gunner with a shotgun and a pistol in reserve. At least you know they will fire.

You will figure out this war stuff like you've figured out everything else though, right? War is just another problem to decipher. You will plan for everything, every contingency. Insurgents right? Spin. Insurgents left? Spin. Rear and front? You've got it covered. You are feeling more confident now. You will communicate with the other gunners with small, handheld Motorola Talkabout radios from the PX and hope the Iraqis are not listening in. You will sip water from the hydration system on your back. You will eat and sleep in your turret. It is your perch, your domain, your battle station, your fiefdom. When it is time to move out, you will be ready.

And then you are. You rack the bolt carrier assemblies back on your M249 Squad Automatic Weapon and the 9mm Beretta pistol strapped to your chest and inject live rounds into their chambers. You rack five Remington slugs into your Mossberg and you strap it to your turret hatch. Your water hydration system is full and you have pieces of your favorite MRE in your butt-pack in case you get hungry. You have your desert-issue goggles and your Oakley sunglasses on and your Surefire tactical flashlight at the close ready for signaling. You do radio checks with the other gunners in the platoon and wish them Godspeed. You play U2's *All That You Can't Leave Behind* CD in the portable player jammed into your CamelBak, and you're ready.

The sun rises as bright and glorious and furious as it has every day since you've been in this desert. The morning air is still relatively cool with a slight breeze. The sky is a stunning shade of blue you had never bothered to appreciate before. The vast openness of the desert sands seems far softer and cleaner than when you first saw it.

The truck engines gurgle and sputter to life. Radios crackle. The familiar smell of engine exhaust and sweaty bodies permeates the air. You give your rear gunner the "rock and roll" hand sign and flash him a grin. Nervous bravado. And then you're moving forward. Forward to the Iraqi border and the line of demarcation.

Allawi

llawi, Allawi, Allawi . . . I hear it still, cutting across the din of the market. It is a place of employment maybe. Or worship. Or school. I wonder what or where Allawi is. Or who. Allawi is lost perhaps. Or missing. I say a quick prayer for Allawi, whatever it may be. In Baghdad, Allawi might be anything. I have no idea. Allawi might be my sanity.

It doesn't take much for me to be back there. Even now, fourteen years later. Every crowd or traffic jam, every shopping mall or bus stop, every queue at any place at any time, I am reminded of it, the market. When people talk about war, when I hear veterans talking about their wars, and I think about my war, I think about that market. I think about Allawi. It is the place I dream of. The place of nightmares.

The street through the market is so hot it scorches the soles of our cheap, army-issued boots. So hot, the discarded innards from the sheep carcasses steam off the pavement and the stench hangs in the air, putrid and alkaline, clinging to our nostrils long into the night. The old men and boys tasked with the slaughtering draw their knives across the throats of doomed, wide-eyed beasts, glimpses of silver from flimsy blades glinting in the sun; slick red blood dripping raw from their hands and between their fingers, clotting and bubbling around their plastic Chinese sandals and fake Adidas trainers. The dull black of our machine guns and rifles and shotguns and pistols is a thin wall around us, its mortar our bristling ammunition belts and columns of green- and orange-tipped rounds pressed into gray magazines and olive-drab pods, shells of Remington buckshot rattle loose in our pockets like handfuls of small stones. We pull the stocks tight into our shoulders, clinging to them like lovers; hard butts of rubber and plastic, grafted with dark steel and smelling of gun oil and cordite. Forged in America, and Germany, and Italy, comforting and horrifying, nylon slings wrapped around clenched fists like prayer beads, nerves and trigger springs together coiled tight, eyes unflinching for fear of blinking.

In the market outside Baghdad International Airport, I stared dully through the cracked, mud-streaked windshield of a banged-up Humvee. Weary but still alert, my eyes absorbed the empty, trash-strewn street. I was tired of it. Every goddamned day, patrolling this godforsaken market, sunup to sundown. Keep the convoys moving through. Push the crowds back. Back. Further back. Keep the roadway clear, at least two lanes' worth of real estate. An endless and futile effort, like sweeping sand off a beach. I thought of the beaches back home. Low tide, high tide; but here the beach was just a dusty street and here the waves were human. Waves of people spilling and tumbling over each other; a demented desperate sea of people, the worst kind, the kind that would surely try to drown you in their wake given the chance, pulling you under, clawing at your straps and body armor and rigging. *Mister, mister, give me dollar.* Pushing and begging. *Chai, mister? You need chai?* Fighting and trampling and grasping over each other. I sipped tepid black coffee from an aluminum canteen cup.

I did not dislike this time of day. I had time enough to ponder but not too much time, not enough to get all nostalgic. Early mornings were almost peaceful. Before the thud of the Black Hawks and Apaches would return overhead and the groans of the Bradley fighting vehicles and Abrams tanks would reverberate through the streets, the market slept. Before the sun would rise over the remnants of the date palm groves along the airport road, when the first rays of light would begin flickering through the charred leviathans, the sparse survivors with trunks scarred and blackened, all was quiet. While the dew still lingered on the aluminum skins of the parked Toyota minibuses, the multicolored taxis, and ancient Mercedes-Benz lorries, the market was at peace.

It never lasted long. The wailings of the muezzins' prayers would soon echo through the labyrinth of empty stalls, waking man and beast now asleep under flimsy metal card tables and wooden carts soon to be weighed down with the precarious livelihoods of so many. A robbery or a murder, a light till or an errant bomb—entire families could be ruined in an instant. How anyone could sleep in this city was beyond me. Though some could not and were already awake. A doctor now compelled to sell parts stripped from a prized BMW. A widow, once whole, now compelled to sell parts of herself. They stood like statues of ancient lives long past, silent, hoping, and ashamed of what they had mustered up the courage to do. Between desperation and survival, there is a distinct absence of dignity. And I was ashamed to bear witness to this.

In moments like these I hated the market and wanted to not be there at all. I hated it with the same force that I loved the sheer defiance of my being there. I *had* to be there. So, I would be there. Because the army said I would be, mostly. It's too hot to care really. The mind wanders.

Allawi, Allawi, Allawi . . . I dream Allawi is in the turret, hunched over the stock of a short-barreled machine gun, eyes scanning the roofs of the sand-colored buildings on our periphery. Sporadic shots fired at the patrol ahead of ours and the longer sustained bursts of return fire from the tanker scout ahead of us interrupt the relative afternoon calm.

Allawi kicks the back of the driver's seat and shouts down for the driver to step on the gas. Move, move, move! Get this fucker moving! Don't get stuck in the kill zone! And the driver floors it, the truck lurching forward towards the gunfire through the traffic. Smoke billows from a vehicle that has been hit by an explosive device and disabled in the intersection ahead, flames belching from its blackened underbelly as its fuel ignites and the thin fiberglass-and-canvas skin begins to melt and peel. Covering fire. The only rounds we ever fired in Iraq were covering fire. Allawi fired them really. Allawi is my guardian angel maybe. Allawi is the angel of death.

Allawi says that the next morning you will wake as if that is the first day you have been on the earth—to savor the crisp, cool morning air, the warmth of the sun on your face, the smell of the charcoal and meat from the kebab stands, the grit of dust in your teeth, the sounds of the bus drivers calling their fares, the voices and feet of little school children contrasting with the rumble of tanks and the vibration of helicopters above them, the taste of cordite and hot gun oil left on your lips after the firing of a machine gun—there is no greater feeling than the realization that one is still alive. Allawi sees this, he says. Allawi says I'm seeing things.

Mostly I see the market from the rear right seat of our unarmored fiberglass-skinned truck. As the day wears on, I would blink the sleep out of my eyes and light another knockoff Marlboro, inhaling its dry, chemical smoke. When I exhale, I aim the blue-tinged cloud up at the turret hatch, partly out of boredom, mostly to annoy my gunner, partly to see if the kid is awake. He throws an empty Pepsi can back down at me in response, no words needed. And we would listen for the sounds of the market stirring. The yelps of a startled dog, a restless donkey's bray, a rooster crowing, a small child crying on a distant rooftop, these are the earliest sounds, small reminders of humanity around us. We would listen for the sound of the radio, for the lieutenant to give the order, breathe in the smell of burning garbage, its acrid wafts drifting lazily upwards in the early morning humidity, and of unwashed bodies and sweat-soaked gear, of days-on-end worn uniforms, stale cigarettes, and half-eaten rations languishing in tattered plastic olive-drab packets.

Soon the smell of charcoal would be in the air from the small fires lit by the tea sellers to boil water in copper pots. The smell of lamb kebabs and chickens roasting on spits would hit the air only to be overwhelmed by the smells of mechanized transport, of petrol and diesel, of burning radiator coolant and hot engine oil and overheated rotors and brake pads. The smell of fear, too, would be in the air. And too soon, after another hot, restless night, it would be time for me to go back into the market, again to this strange waltz in the sun. Soon Baghdad would awake completely, its merchants and residents intermingling among the stalls and tables, among the decrepit plastic chairs and dusty piles of bricks, the rickety horse carts, shells of bombed out cars, and bent frames of rusted bicycles and battered motorcycles. One step forward, two steps back; the market would expand like a tempest, intent on surging forward, on swallowing the roadway running through its center, swelling the sea onto a shallow beach, drowning, consuming, devouring, and killing us, erasing our very existence.

"Are you awake, Sergeant?" the private asks from above. We are waiting by the roundabout for the crackle of the radio, for the cursed transmission that sends us back in. We are in a nightmare, the one where the room grows smaller and smaller until we are crushed to death. We are at the bottom of a newly dug grave and wait for the earth to rain down on our faces. The market wants to swallow us alive; every cell and organism within it rebels against our presence there. The market wants only to consume and expel us. We are in its center, foreign, intrusive. We are a cancer, a gaping raw wound the market wants only to close. And beneath the noise of commerce, the market buzzes its hatred of us like a nest of provoked and angry wasps.

I check the lanyard on my pistol one last time, flick the safety off, black to red. I rack a slug into my shotgun. Then I step out of the truck and into the market. Toward the cries of *Allawi, Allawi, Allawi* . . . always, always *Allawi*.

Bluebeard Of Baghdad

War makes for bad fairytales. When my daughter asks me what I did in the war, what the war was about, I will tell her a "war story" in the form of a fairytale maybe. A war fairytale that could have been derived from a storybook because of its sheer absurdity. Places where evil kings and princes and heroic knights of all sorts meet and do battle, like in fairytales. And so, I remember it sometimes in these ways. In stories, or fables, of sorts.

Such as this one:

In Baghdad there was a wealthy and powerful prince. As heir to the throne, the prince indulged himself in every luxury his position afforded him. Throughout Mesopotamia, many tales were told about the splendor of the prince's palaces, his horses, carriages, and treasures, and of his great, long tables laden with all manner of fowl, beast, fruit, and wine, and all that the prince desired. The prince took great pride in having the finest linens, silver and gold timepieces, and distilled spirits, brought to him by couriers from kingdoms spanning every corner of the earth. While the indulgences of his father were not small by any measure, those of the prince made those of the king seem as miniscule and as distant as one of his falcons circling high above the highest of minarets. Although his father was known to be a cruel tyrant, the prince promised to be crueler than his father, and the word of his cruelty sowed a deep, growing despair within the hearts of his people.

Of all the things the prince lusted for, he had one desire that could never be satisfied: the adoration of women. But the prince did not just want the love of any women, as he had a wife and several concubines. He wanted to be adored by all of the finest and most beautiful women in the city. For as Baghdad was his, so would be its women. They would be his to conquer, possess, consume, and discard. His henchmen scoured the streets in search of more and ever more women for the prince, seizing them from the streets of their villages, and from the tranquility of their universities, and from the sanctity of their homes. And if they did not adore him willingly because he gave them fine things, the prince would use his power and ruthlessness to wrest from them every last gasp of fealty that they might utter with their final breath.

Wives, daughters, sisters, virgins—the prince's lust could never be satisfied. He defiled them all, ignoring their pleas and their cries, and the pleas and cries of their husbands and fathers and brothers and lovers. Even the wives of his most loyal praetorians were not to be exempted from their service to the prince. For if his own men refused him their wives, the prince would make them watch as he tortured them. Beautiful faces and elegant necks would be slashed by daggers. Painted nails were torn away and hennaed hands crushed and mangled. Long, soft hair would be set aflame and smooth skin blackened and scorched. Arms and torsos and thighs and legs were bruised and pulverized by a thousand blows from clubs and whips and the blunt ends of a hundred sabers. Shattered bodies were slathered with sticky honey from the prince's beehives, and at the foot of his bed chambers, and in his gardens, and in his jails wild dogs would strip the flesh from their bones.

Because of his cruelty, the prince had many enemies, and the Lions of the 15 Shaaban were chief amongst them. These Lions sought vengeance upon him for the lives of their wives and their daughters and their sisters and for themselves and for their honor and for the great dark stain of blood on the prince's hands and the flesh of their women rotting in the distended bellies of the prince's dogs and within the rusted sarcophagus of the prince's iron maiden. The Lions mourned as more and more of their women were sacrificed at the altar of the prince's lust; and they plotted against him, lying in wait in dark places for their moment to strike.

On a December evening, just after dusk, this moment was given to them in the market of Mansour where the most beautiful and wealthy of Baghdad's women were known to gather. The prince was riding in one of the finest of his carriages—and he was unguarded.

Four Lions were concealed within the market of Mansour on that night, as they had been every night, hidden amongst the shopkeepers and street peddlers. They had been waiting for weeks upon weeks, night after night, hour upon hour, waiting and watching, praying to the Prophet for one opportunity to exact their vengeance upon the prince. And when they saw him, emboldened by the cover of darkness–having dispatched his henchmen on an errand–the Lions were astounded by their good fortune. They knew on this night that this was the moment for which they had waited so long. They poured fire into the carriage, piercing its armor and fine leathers, shattering its glass portals, and gravely wounding the prince with molten lead as sharp as the sharpest of sabers, until they were certain that the prince was dead.

But he was not quite dead even then. Seventeen wounds did the prince sustain at the hands of the Lions. Impaled throughout his head and neck, his arms and legs, his torso and spine, and deep into his loins, it was said by those who would still dare to speak against the prince, that he was no more man than eunuch.

The Lions of the 15 Shaaban could do little more than flee the prince's wrath, for they were few and his men were many. His power and cruelty were as vast as the desert west of the Euphrates and his thirst for vengeance after the attempt on his life was multiplied one-thousandfold by the pain from his still festering wounds. The prince and his henchmen and his dogs hunted the Lions all throughout the streets and markets of Baghdad, to the marshes of Suq ash-Shuyukh near the banks of the river Tigris, to every distant village and dark corner of the country. As far away as Persia, the Lions were hunted by the prince. And when they were found, many a Lion would die horribly at the prince's hands for their crime. Their houses were burned, their possessions were seized, their fathers and brothers and sons were struck down by fire and saber, and their mothers and sisters and wives were imprisoned. He gave no quarter. He showed no mercy. Until the memory of the Lions' stand on that ill-fated night in Mansour was as distant as the stars in the infinite night sky.

Several years would pass before mention of the Lions would be heard again in Baghdad. The rumors started as a faint hum. Softly at first, then louder until it was as loud as the anguished screams of the damned emitting from the bowels of the prince's darkest prisons. Word circulated throughout the land from the poorest village to the prince's palace: the Lions had formed a league with a savage people from the New World. It was said that these savage people held great dominion over the use of fire in warfare, and possessed countless sabers forged from the hardest of metals, and impenetrable armored carriages, and vast battalions of savage warriors numbering in the thousands upon thousands. Hearing this, the prince feared for his life, and he barricaded himself inside of a villa owned by his kinsman far north of Baghdad, in the old city of Mosul.

The Lions led the warriors of the New World to the prince's doorstep. Their arrival shook the walls of the villa with the great and horrible rumblings of their war machines. The prince trembled in terror knowing that his fate was inevitable, his hands forever stained by the blood of Baghdad's innocents. Impotent against the fury of the warrior assault, the prince cowered, hiding among the battered corpses of his own lifeless men, and among those, his brother, and his brother's beloved son, until the prince was certain that he would surely drown in all of their blood.

When they found him, the warriors of the New World took great pleasure in firing into the prince projectile after molten projectile; again, and again—until his blood poured from him like that which poured from the veins of those he disposed of like so little chattel. It was a good kill, a righteous one, as there could be no other justice befitting the prince's crimes than to die badly. In Baghdad, within the walls of the prince's gardens, American soldiers rejoiced in the shadows of the prince's iron maidens. Soon renderings of the prince's ruined corpse and the stories of his death would be sent to every corner of every kingdom on earth as a warning to those who might resist the Great Crusade. And unlike the blood shed by Baghdad's beauty, and that of the prince's dissenters, his resisters, and the Lions who risked everything for the promise of nothing—for dignity—all that was left of the prince lay bloated and congealed in the Baghdad dust.

Of course, this is not a fairytale. This is a war story. And my daughter, who was six months old then, is a girl of sixteen now who does not care about either fairytales or war stories. It turns out that this is just how I want to remember it. This is how I tell the story to myself.

Medevac

War is hell. War is grotesque. War is obscene. Tim O'Brien, quintessential Vietnam War veteran writer, says that a true war story makes the stomach turn. A true war story embarrasses you. You think that this is a good assessment of war stories.

In your own true war story, you are standing guard at the 270th Armor's perimeter gate off Baghdad's Highway 10, fighting to keep your eyes open, staring off into the dark nothingness of the evening sky. Having overslept the night before last and showed up late to relieve your squad leader, you had volunteered to cover his next shift in addition to your own after a long day of patrols. Screwing your superior out of a well-deserved night's sleep is not one of the most prudent of things to do in the army so taking an extra duty was your best reprieve. Self-inflicted punishment is often easier to swallow than that which comes from above.

Halfway through the second watch, all the Abrams tanks and Bradley Fighting Vehicles are in for the night, the imams have finished their evening wailings, and you are counting down the hours with a PFC from the tankers whose name you don't recall. You're not even sure if you even asked for it at the time. To you he is just another nameless, faceless, skinny tanker kid from the South, not much of a talker, which you appreciate, and to him you are just another nameless, faceless military police sergeant from the North. After this night, you will probably see each other only once or twice more or never again anyway. No point getting all familiar with anyone on the night shift. It will be some six hours or so until your reliefs roll out of their cots and stumble groggily onto the dirt track toward your position. You just sit there, intermittently smoking Chinese cigarettes and staring out into the street, watching the insects swarm around the flickering street lights. Bored.

When skinny tanker kid's shift was near its end, you let him go on back to his hooch to wake up his replacement, not seeing the point of holding him over any longer than necessary, knowing he probably had a full day of patrols to get through after this. At least he would catch a few hours of sleep and the sooner the better. Except the goddamn kid either never woke up his replacement or his replacement just rolled over and went back to sleep and no relief ever came.

Now generally this wouldn't be an issue. You would have radioed into the TOC and informed the duty sergeant of the situation and they would have sent someone out. Except no one is answering the radio in the TOC, and they never send anyone out either. In a situation like this, no communications, the reliefs too far away to get to without abandoning your post, all you can do is maintain position. Worse comes to worst, an Iraqi breaches the wire, you light them up with a 30-round mag of 5.56 and a 15-round clip of 9mm. Someone at that point had better come running, duty sergeant, QRF, the Estonian Special Operations Force, anyone supposed to already be inside the wire.

So that is Plan A, the only plan actually until your stomach began contracting, contorting, making horrific-sounding noises like a demon spawn trying to abort itself through your bowel. Cramping like you have never experienced in your lifetime. And the thought instantly flashes through your head: massive food poisoning. The roadside kebabs from the market maybe. The hot rations from earlier in the day. The malaria pills. The anthrax vaccines. Who knows what the fuck. But something, anything, whatever it was, it is coming out quick and with a vengeance.

Plan B is decided for you. You have to drop trou and can't hold inside whatever is about to come out for a second longer. Nor do you dare make a run for the Porta-shitter and risk leaving the wire unmanned. So, there you are, in a full-out squat, M16 rifle on the ground in front of you, DCU trousers around your ankles, foul chemical-smelling blood and mucous and shit running out your now-bare ass in greasy dark streams into the still-simmering burn pit full of trash, just out of sight of the road where you can still see the thin strands of concertina wire separating you from the rest of Baghdad. An M9 9mm Beretta pistol in your left hand, a round in the chamber, you use your right–now devoid of all dignity–to spray water down your crotch from your

CamelBak, defiling your woodland camouflage bandana in a futile attempt to clean yourself. Then, absent any other options, you stuff it deep down into the pile of steaming blood, guts, and shit until it disappears.

Defend the gate at all costs, they said. Dignity is cheap, they said. It's the army's first general order, for Christ's sake. The first order a boot private learns in basic. "I will guard everything within the limits of my post and quit my post only when properly relieved." *Properly relieved*, you think. Ha. How's this for properly relieved. Or *quitting* your post. There is no quitting. There is only squatting bare-assed in the dark and trying not to fall over backwards into a steaming cesspool of human feces, rotting food, flesh, chemicals, boxes, and God knows what else people have been burning.

It is a long fucking night. Dawn breaks, the morning prayers are called, the Abrams tanks and Bradley Fighting Vehicles head back out to make their first sweeps for IEDs, the morning replacements finally arrive. You manage to shuffle back to the platoon area to give yourself a proper scrubbing before the water is too hot from the morning sun and to see the platoon medic.

Blood, you say. Lots of blood and guts and shit, you say. The medic refers you to the battalion doctor, one of those perpetually sweating, near-obese Reserve officers, and he puts you on a combination of antibiotics and steroids with instructions to drink plenty of water. "Yes sir, thank you, sir," you say, and for the next month or so you do exactly that while having the same bouts of crazed shitting and bleeding with no improvement.

For its part, the army does what it can for you in Baghdad. Your squad gamely convoys up to the CSH at Camp Anaconda in Balad more than a few times to see the doctors there. You take medevac choppers from the BIAP to the same place and hitch rides back to Baghdad on the back of deuce-and-a-halfs.

One crew of two cooks from a field kitchen, having been held up without a convoy escort, needed a gunner on board to get cleared for road travel. "We got the clearance?" you asked from the back of the open-air truck bed. The private grinned as he climbed up into the driver's seat. "Shit yeah, Sarn't. I told 'em we got an MP in the back with a SAW and a pistol." And off you went, on the highway south to Baghdad, two army cooks and an MP sergeant with bleeding guts, a stack of empty Mermite containers, and an M249 SAW light machine gun bumping around in the back, clinging to the camo netting of a decrepit soft-top cargo truck hoping to make it back without getting shot or shitting yourself.

❦

You come home from Baghdad earlier than you'd planned. Not with your platoon mates, not alongside your brothers and sisters in arms. There are no red-white-and-blue flags snapping in the spring New England breeze at the Armory, no crowds cheering or dignitaries there to shake your hand. You are not wounded by enemy fire or an explosion. There are no glorious stories of battles hard fought and blood spilt behind walls of dust-colored bricks and stone. You are no Lawrence of Arabia, no conquering hero of the wars in the Middle East that have long stretched our economy and snuffed out the lives of thousands. You come home in the fall of 2003 when your battalion medical officer dispatches you to Kuwait on a C-130 medevac flight with a mere, "I'm obligated to send you stateside for treatment, Sergeant." And that is the beginning of the end of your part in the Iraq war.

From Kuwait, it is on to a flight to Ramstein Air Force Base in Germany and then Landstuhl and finally Kaiserslautern where you and your fellow med-evacuees will be billeted for a time. On the bus to Landstuhl, the air force tech-sergeant passes around cold beers for the ride. More than a few of you show up for your first medical appointments more than a little buzzed, having not really drunk in months, setting the stage for what will be most of your time in Germany.

Debauchery soon prevails over military discipline. As it happens, life in and around Kaiserslautern is a near free-for-all for the walking wounded. With almost no military police left in the country, the civilian police and security guards manning the gates could care less about what time anyone wanders in for the night. And without the presence of one's chain of command, you soon discover there isn't anyone keeping track of when anyone arrives or leaves.

For many reservists and National Guardsmen, a ticket to Walter Reed in Washington, DC, means your war is over. You will be released from active duty and sent home to your respective states. Active duty soldiers on the other hand are in a much different boat. They are either going to medical holding companies at bases scattered throughout the U.S. or back to their units in Iraq or Afghanistan, and they are in no hurry for either of those options. You meet one active duty soldier who has found a girlfriend and started working as a bartender in town, only checking in to medical appointments from time to time so as not to appear totally AWOL.

In Kaiserslautern, you spend two weeks indulging in hot showers, drinking copious amounts of pilsner with wounded tankers and Marines, absorbing the alcohol with pretzels and bratwurst, and trying to figure out what to do next. One moment you were smoking shisha on a Baghdad rooftop and the next you are stumbling drunk, singing marching cadences with rowdy Texans and getting dragged out of clubs by the Polizei. It is the most culture-shocked one can get, all that booze and porn, zero supervision, and slurred, one-sided conversations with German bar girls who mostly want to be anywhere else but talking to the drunken bands of sexually frustrated, tanned, and tattooed servicemen newly returned to the western world. When you finally do decide to go home after you can't drink any more beer and the doctors can't do anything more for you in Germany, you board a massive air force plane loaded with stretchers and rows of soldiers, Marines, airmen, and crates of more beer, all on their way stateside. The flight crew serves hot dogs and warm cookies in-flight, and you remember the smell to this day, a distinctly American smell, like the Fourth of July, and Walmart.

You finish out your army enlistment at Walter Reed Medical Center. Assigned to a medical holding company, you take your place among a menagerie of malingerers, certifiable psychos, and the genuinely sick and wounded. Many of them single- or double-amputees, they struggle to navigate this new battlefield of curbs and hills and stairways. Muscling their wheelchairs through the snow, their eyes peering through their often burned and shrapnel-scarred faces, their skin exposed as summer uniforms not designed to accommodate the stump of a missing leg or an arm betray their flesh to the cold winter air.

Poked and prodded and stuck with needles, and IV catheters pumping into your veins, you wonder how anyone would ever be so stupid or suicidal as to provoke a war with the United States. What was Saddam thinking? Did he even know he was doing it? And what cruel God would now make you live through this hell? As if it were your fault the war was an absolute fraud. With little to do besides your individual medical appointments, those of you who are more mobile spend your days contemplating the answers to such questions, going to movies, wandering about the museums and memorials, getting plastered in hotel bars, and sometimes just sitting alone in the hospital chapel.

You will be standing in the formation of the Medical Holding Company one afternoon when an orderly comes running to escort you to the hospital lobby with other Connecticut Guardsmen who have begun filtering in from Baghdad. One sergeant has to have a cancerous mass cut out of his head. Your company's captain has shrapnel in his arm. A private had part of his foot blown off, and a specialist has a plate screwed into his skull. But since the state's adjutant general has arrived with a *Hartford Courant* reporter, a public affairs officer is intent on trotting out everyone who can for a photo-op. In the end, it ends up just being you and the wounded private though. "Connecticut is proud of you", the general says. "I'm proud of you. You're all *heroes*." Beaming with grandfatherly pride, he smiles widely for the cameras as he presents each of you with his two-star challenge coins and some woodland camouflage winter Gortex jackets to accompany your desert-issue BDUs. The reporter and an army public affairs sergeant are excitedly scribbling down the story unfolding before their eyes. Connecticut's *heroes* in the flesh. Amazing. You get it though. Nutmeggers don't get out much.

"Take care of your men, Sergeant."

"Yes, sir, hooah, sir. Say hello to the folks back home for us, sir," you mutter halfheartedly in the direction of the old man and his entourage as they beat a hasty retreat back to the mother state.

You and the private just look at each other in stunned silence. It is a dog and pony show. One of you is the dog and the other the pony. You ask him if he needs anything like a good sergeant would, but he just shakes his head and turns his coin over in his hand with that same puzzled look. He might still be in shock over his entire ordeal, or it might be the pain meds. Or he might be wondering who you are since you don't remember meeting him until that day. You had been in different platoons after all. Anyway, you stop in to check on him a few times while you are both still there until one day there is a new private in his room.

The army discharges you and sends you home in May 2004. It is like you have been asleep for a year and everything and nothing has changed. That is to say that everything within you has changed while nothing on the outside has even budged. At restaurants and bars and malls and parks and beaches, Iraq's invasion and occupation might as well have not happened. It was just a thing that flickered across the television screen from time to time, reminding people of their fellow citizens losing their lives and limbs instead of them. And for what? No one really seems to think much about that either.

The Fat Sergeant Major

At the head of the column trots the fat sergeant-major. It is queer that almost all of the regular sergeant-majors are fat. Himmelstoss follows him, thirsting for vengeance. His boots gleam in the sun. . . . Then he steams off with Himmelstoss in his wake.

—Ernst, in *All Quiet on the Western Front*

Himmelstoss, as anyone knows who is familiar with the story in *All Quiet on the Western Front*, is the sadistic corporal who bullies and torments those he outranks. The fat sergeant major, whose girth underscores his lavish and immoderate lust for comfort while the rank-and-file tighten their belts in the trenches, is happy to be the weight behind Himmelstoss's threats. As Paul Bäumer's character recounts, he and the other soldiers immediately disregard both Himmelstoss and the fat sergeant-major, continuing on no worse for the wear.

We've all had a Himmelstoss in our lives at one time or another. They're school principals and executive vice presidents and postal deliverymen and yes, sergeants major. Some are fat. And the thing is, one should not dwell on men like these for any more time than they are in our direct presence. I came across one during my time spent at Walter Reed Army Medical Center on my way home from Iraq. "Where is your beret, Sergeant?" the Medical Corps sergeant major, who had halted me on my way to an appointment, said, "And why are you wearing a desert patrol cap with a woodland uniform?" Thinking it obvious, I respectfully informed the sergeant major that my beret was still in a conex in the desert. "Put that cigarette out, sergeant, and stand at parade rest when you speak to me. And don't you dare throw that cigarette butt in my grass," the sergeant major said. His posture was threatening, though I sensed behind it the existential terror of a man without serious occupation.

What else is one to do in such a situation but put one's cigarette out on the pavement, then collect and squeeze it carefully in one's clenched fist? His wet eyes pleaded with me, begging some minor transgression, so that he might thrust himself upon me further, so that we might enter the kind of seedy and disreputable relationships these types of flaccid human fleshbags always seem to require for satisfaction. At that moment, I was tempted to give it to him, but thought better of it.

"Roger, sergeant," I said. But that wasn't the end of it.

"What's your name? What unit are you with? Who's your C-O? Take that flag off your right shoulder, you're not in theater anymore," he said, his voice picking up speed and certainty as he warmed to the subject. "Desert boots, that's a no-go. Are you wearing a field jacket liner? Ohhhhh heeeeaaaayl naw," he said, his voice rising almost to a full-throated shout.

It was true, I was wearing an old M-65 field jacket liner under my uniform top instead of the newer-issue winter polypropylene. "Yes, Sergeant Major, I will remove it, Sergeant Major," I said, standing corrected, quite literally, in the brisk winter air. I had no intention of removing it, and I didn't. I wore the motherfucker to bed that night. Hell, I'm still wearing that thing, deep in the recesses of the old footlocker that keeps my mementos of such places, stinking of smoke and dust and sweat and bullshit.

Whether you're still in the military, have transitioned into the corporate world, or are a civilian and have never served, it's always the same. An FSM is lurking, waiting to gig you on some stupid, asinine shit. It is something we all must face, and disregard, with a smile and a nod and a "Yes, Sergeant Major" or "Vice President" or "Foreman." Because that is all they will ever be—the barking, savage whiff of authority barely missed, one step below or behind the boss. Forever the bridesmaid, never the bride. And after you realize that, what else do they have left to them but the illusion of power, usually shouted? They're stuck within this sad, diminished aura, a victim of their penultimate rank. Give them "their grass" for the moment, or "their metrics" at close of business, or "their tie rods" in even rows in the next hour, and then go home. Or travel. Or go to school. Or anything. Somewhere I have a photo of an army cargo truck in Baghdad with "Stop the Insanity" scrawled across its passenger door. Sometimes that's all we can do to remind ourselves who is really in charge and continue our idiosyncratic lives, one graffitied door at a time.

I never saw that particular sergeant major again, thankfully. I supposed he moved on to harass other troops about their shoulder patches until the regulation was changed a month later. I would have loved to see his face the morning after the paper came down, applying the patch he'd fought so hard against with resignation, then instructing the soldiers he'd yelled at the day before to get within regs . . . admitting his own impotence one betrayal at a time.

Since then, there have been other FSMs who have thrown their "stripes" around in the various settings in which I have worked. Though, now that I think about it, when has it ever really mattered to anyone but them? We the people remain unimpressed. In the Vietnam War film *Hamburger Hill*, a couple of troops try and buck up their platoon "Doc" after a casualty, chanting, "It don't mean nothing, man, not a thing." And the medic, thus consoled and encouraged, goes on to fight another day. We all have bad days like Doc in the film. That sergeant major I met long ago now might have been having a bad day too. In the end, it really doesn't mean a thing. Doc doesn't survive the battle. He succumbs to his wounds after imploring his fellow soldiers to finish taking the hill, so they can have something to be proud of. And they do. They do it for Doc and for each other. Those are the things that matter.

LUST

The breathless wonder, the impetuousness, the night wind, the darkness, the questionings—all those things that were still with us when, as sixteen-year-old boys, we would race along after Adele and the other girls through the flickering, gas-lit wind—these never came back. Though the time was when the woman was not a whore, yet it did not come back; though I believed it might still be otherwise, and though she embraced me and I trembled with desire, yet it did not come back. —Afterwards I was always wretched.

—Erich Maria Remarque, *The Road Back*

Before

This is me. Before. The place where my sisters and I grew up is a small Connecticut town, Glastonbury, just southeast of Hartford. As a child I longed to see beyond the fences of that little town and the towns beyond those, the oceans, and the cities, and the deserts, as far as my eyes could see, and as long as my legs would carry me. Every day there only made me more restless, made me think more about the world I was missing, the sights I was not seeing, the smells, the tastes, the wonders of the unknown and satisfaction of conquering the unexplored, until I was nearly blind with the urge to run away. I was only three when I made my first break for it, ready to go at the first opportunity. I saw an open door and headed off, running across the yard and making it almost to the street before being picked up by a passing postman. At ten I discovered the joys of wheeled transportation, pedaling for miles on my secondhand bicycle until I was hungry and tired enough to turn around and pedal back home.

At the end of a cul-de-sac just behind the baseball fields, I lived in a two-story house with my four sisters and parents. I never played Little League baseball simply because there was no money for those things, but I did enjoy watching it and spent many hours in the window doing so. There was a small television and plenty of books, but not much else for entertainment. There were no pets, of the cat or dog type, but the occasional rodent or fish would cycle through its short life behind the walls of a glass cage or aquarium from time to time, each one loved and cared for by their five young attendants.

The houses in our neighborhood were mostly three- and four-bedroom boxes with aluminum skin built in endless rows. They were originally constructed to shelter laborers for Pratt and Whitney Aircraft during World War II, but when I was a boy they housed the children of Vietnam War veterans, and generations of poor Hispanics, Blacks, the elderly, and the sick. Haggard single parents working nights, housewives tired from carting groceries and children the mile into town, ragged project kids, aimless, who fought each other often, and with great joy I fought amongst them.

The best thing about being a child and poor, is that being poor means very little to you. The only people who care that you are poor are those who are not so poor. Sometimes the church folks would come around dropping off boxes of canned food and the old ladies with their concerned faces and stuffy noses would shake our hands and give us hard candies. We certainly had enough peanut butter and powdered milk. It was not a bad beginning, humble as it was. It is only as you grow older that you become aware of what being poor really means and that being poor sucks. But when we were small, my sisters and I were happy enough with our secondhand clothes, secondhand bicycles, secondhand books, and the occasional new toy that would appear on our birthdays or at Christmas. When you are young and poor, it is much easier to dream.

I did not attend school as a child. I spent my days in the aluminum box of a house, with my sisters for classmates, one day studying history, one day studying science, engaged in what is now called by some in this country as alternative learning. What it felt like though was a prison sentence, and my only true escape was the window of the written word, my teachers the dusty shadows in stale corners of the Welles Turner Library. In my younger years, I was primarily self-taught. The town library was just a ten-minute bicycle ride away on Main Street, near the old bank building and the fountain where the people would toss their pocket change. There, I could be found almost daily within the stacks, fighting battles alongside great generals, exploring new lands with the great explorers, and traversing vast and desolate deserts with sheiks and princes. No one interrupted me, and I interrupted no one. No one asked why I was not in school, and so I never wondered. In Connecticut, people tend to keep to themselves.

Eventually I would return home at the end of the day, often with a new pile of biographies and old novels, those library editions with the musty smell and the stained, industrial hardcovers that could stop a bullet. I would read late into the night by flashlight, a habit I would find both useful as a soldier and hard to break long after. But as a child, I would dream of those faraway places after falling asleep, flashlight and book in hand.

When I wasn't dreaming of travel or nose deep in a book, I was off somewhere on that old bicycle, memorizing street names, mapping routes in my head, and imagining I was on some important adventure. I quickly discovered that I possessed a keen sense of direction and a talent for estimating my location off the images of the maps I held in my head. Later on, I would check the actual maps in the blue pages of our phone books to see how far I'd gone, where I had been, and where I might venture on my next foray into the unknown. These days, kids have Google Maps on their cellphones. But that's not nearly as much fun as paper maps.

❖

I like to tell people I was raised by wolves. I ate scraps for food and clung to my siblings for warmth in our cold little den, howling at the moon. This is, of course, too ridiculous to be true.

The real story is that I am the firstborn son of an immigrant soccer-playing, Chilean housepainter and an American-born depressive deli clerk. We were Mormons while my parents were together; after my father left us, my mother was a Mormon no longer. She remarried two years later, this time to a fundamentalist Baptist and Vietnam veteran. These Baptists were more wolves than sheep, and they preyed on each other, the unwitting, the weak within their flock, and on the occasional unfortunate who had stumbled into their trap out of a combination of curiosity and bad luck.

I remember very little of my real father. What I know of him has been told to me by my mother or relayed through siblings over the years. What I have come to understand is that I was better off without him then, and still today. When I think of my father I no longer feel shame, or regret, or fear, or anger. What I feel is sadness, and not for me, but for him.

He is a religious man, apparently, a Mormon convert upon arriving on American soil. He left when I was three, the second of my mother's husbands to beat feet, this time leaving two more children for my mother as a consolation. We languished in the East Hartford projects until she fell in with the Baptists. My father, though, didn't waste any time, soon taking up with a nurse from his Mormon congregation who would become his next wife and my half-brother's mother. He stuck around with his new family for a few more years before leaving them too, to move out west, closer to the Tabernacle so central to his faith. Eventually he settled in California, married his third American wife, and they produced even more children, both sons and daughters, fulfilling their religious duty to "be fruitful and multiply and replenish the earth." These sons and daughters, as I've been informed through the modern grapevine of social media, are particularly involved in the activities of the Church of the Latter Days, well on their way to sainthood through their good works.

On occasion when I am feeling particularly benevolent, I may feel some remorse for my father, that he never knew my sister and me, or our half-brother, with whom we have grown close. I am sad that my father will never know the adults we have grown into, meet who we married, or the children we had, all without him. He never knew a father's pride at watching his sons march in the uniform of the country that gave him refuge and opportunities, and he will never point us out in a picture to his friends and say, "You see that there? Those are my two sons. One was with the US Army in Iraq and one in Afghanistan." That is all I know of my father. That is all I remember. That is all I care to remember.

My mother . . . well, something was not quite right with my mother in those days. Too often, she seemed to be drowning in something. She became extremely paranoid and lived in fear. She was afraid to send us to public school for fear of my father kidnapping my sister and me and taking us back to Chile. She was afraid to drive a car on the highway. Afraid to own a microwave for fear of radiation exposure from its electric magnetic field. Afraid of us bicycling without a helmet for fear of a fatal concussion on the pavement. Afraid of us playing with sticks or rubber-band guns or anything with a point for fear of us losing an eye, and of us eating food from neighbor's houses for fear of it being contaminated or uncooked. She was afraid for our sight and our hearing and our sense of touch and taste and smell. And of course, she was afraid for our souls. My mother's fears were a large part of my childhood, and eventually I grew so tired of them that I insisted on taking the opposite approach, scaling to the tops of swaying trees and pedaling off on my bicycle for miles.

Now though, I can empathize much more. One's life can become something you never imagined before you realize it. One day it's peace and love in California, and the next you've got five kids and a hamster in government housing.

I do have one happy memory of her that stands out vividly. I must have been about twelve. My sisters and I convinced my mother to ride one of our bicycles around the yard. The bike itself was a sorry contraption, one of those old BMX or Huffy things we'd picked up at a tag sale or traded from one of the other project kids in the neighborhood for a skateboard or a scooter. Until that day, we'd never seen my mother on a bicycle and weren't even sure if she could ride one. I can't remember what inspired the moment or possessed her to take us up on our dare, but she got on the bike and started to pedal. Balancing carefully, a little shaky at first, she laughed nervously then grew more confident, giggling and pedaling furiously in circles around and around the house. Through the patchwork of grass and sand and past the spindly maple tree my stepdad and I had dug up from the side of one of those old country roads in Glastonbury, she pedaled and pedaled as my sisters and I ran after her, shrieking at the absurdity and sheer unabashed exuberance of my mother's triumph. We were amazed and overjoyed and astonished at our mother, her face flushed and girlish, her out-of-breath happy laughter washing away any remnant of her earlier melancholy. That is the mother I would prefer to remember.

But after dinner that same night all went back to normal. It was only a short reprieve from the sadness our life seemed to cause her.

As far as the church was concerned, my mother had been divorced twice and therefore was an adulterer. Although she had been "saved by grace," her sins washed away, my stepfather was barred from any church office such as deacon. Marrying my mother made him an adulterer, too, and my sisters and I the children of adulterers according to the Scripture. Weighed down by her scarlet letter, my mother took her place among those *other* ladies, the ones who silently labored during church dinners scooping dollops of soggy rigatoni and lasagna onto paper plates, or pouring store-brand soda into plastic cups, ladies who murmured quiet prayers in a small sad circle at Wednesday night prayer meetings.

In the summers, my jet-black hair and tanned face clashed with the pale skin and light hair of my half-sisters. In young photos of us, my sisters and I look like refugees. We wore ill-fitting hand-me-down clothes given to us by a family of former Jews for Jesus, and rode to church services and summer revival tent meetings and Vacation Bible schools in the rusted-out, powder blue Ford Econoline my stepfather could barely afford to keep running. I remember him steering and pushing the stalled behemoth, arm through the driver's side window, me outside at the rear, skinny arms and legs outstretched, small muscles taught and straining, face burning crimson, praying desperately, futilely, for the old machine to start up again, just this one last time. Eventually it would, but the result was being almost always late for church services. The Baptists do not look fondly upon the tardy.

My family's sky blue, ancient wreck of a vehicle was both an eyesore and topic of hilarity for my fellow church members. With its gaping rips and tears along its lower sides held together by Bondo, duct tape, and primer, and its belching, blue-tinged exhaust smelling of burning oil and differential fluid, the old van struggled valiantly to ferry us back and forth to church twice on Sundays, to Wednesday night prayer meeting, and to the various youth activities, church picnics, and evangelistic community outreach on Saturdays.

Seven of us, in various stages of equally ratty Sunday attire, would ride in that rattletrap. How we all didn't die in that thing is as close to a holy miracle as I ever witnessed. There was my stepdad in a short-sleeved Oxford with one of those wide-bottomed paisley neckties straight out of a 1970s thrift store. Then there was my mother in a long Little House on the Prairie dress and dreadfully faded striped windbreaker, its once white stripes now a grungy grey, its once purple hue now a sunbaked ghastly brown. There were my four sisters in a hodgepodge of hand-me-down dresses, culottes, tights, knee socks, and shoes with little crooked bows. And then there was me, as much of a mess as the rest of the family, my pants always too big or too tight, my shirts equally ill-fitting, and my shoes scuffed, toes blown out.

Surely, we were the laughingstock of the congregation. At least they gave us the courtesy of mocking us behind our backs. And laugh as they did then, I should have thanked them for the favor they did us. My sisters and I were closer back then because we had to be. Apart from our small circle of equally dirt-poor church friends, my sisters and I spent all of our time together. The neighborhood kids were all away at school most of the day. And given our fundamentalist Baptist tendencies to try and save everyone from everlasting hellfire, most of them were not super keen on hanging out with us much. So, we mainly had each other, my sisters and I, a thing I wish now that I had been more aware of.

I also spent a lot of time on my own. From my small bedroom corner, my desk and floor piled high with stacks of musty library hardcovers, I read until I fell asleep and dreamt of sea captains and soldiers, frontiersmen and explorers, Indian chieftains and warriors, and of great battles fought and distant lands discovered. I triumphed over their victories; I mourned their losses. With little else to do, I drew Revolutionary War battleship after battleship, carefully distinguishing mainmast from foremast, topsails and staysails, riggings and cannons.

One of my favorite ships was the *Bonhomme Richard* captained by John Paul Jones, who had become one of my earliest heroes for his courage during the Battle of Flamborough Head in 1779. I drew this particular ship over and over, and still find myself drawing it from time to time. In pubs on napkins, in the sand in North African wadis, in the condensation on my car windshield. It's kind of weird that I still do it. Or maybe it's the only thing that I've ever learned and can still remember how to draw. And it's stuck with me for so long because I want to see some of myself in Jones and his ship—battered, sinking, but still having only begun to fight.

Preacher Man

"Ask Christ to come into your heart," the preacher said. "Ask him to wash your sins away," he pleaded. But I couldn't move. The auditorium was so hot, stifling in the summer evening despite the open windows and the slow August breeze trickling across the pews.

Others were going forward, but I was paralyzed, limbs frozen in place, begging Jesus for a voice or a sign, anything that would make me believe beyond a shadow of a doubt, waiting for Christ to save me. To count me among the names etched into his Book of Life. A hymn droned on, its slow, torturous ballad, and I prayed that the music would not end. Surely Jesus, who died on the cross for all of us, would answer me. He had to, before the hymn stopped, or I might lose my chance.

Grown men and ladies, young girls and boys, some of them in tears, were still going forward, all of them with heads bowed and hands clasped in desperate, tight knots of shame and repentance, fealty to their God. "Give yourselves over to Jesus now," the preacher was saying, evangelistic fervor in his eyes, raised to the heavens, oblivious to me, the boy in the back pew by the French doors, standing all alone.

The preacher had surely seen that same look before on a thousand other faces throughout the country. From the rolling green mountains and coastal tides of New England to the Bible-belt in the Carolinas and the Deep South, as far west as the Pacific and as far north as the Great Lakes with their bone-chilling snows and soul-sucking winters. He was perspiring now, beads of sweat forming and rolling off his forehead from his hairline to his brow. Spittle formed at the creases and corners of his mouth.

"Come forth, come to Jesus, please come to Jesus," the preacher was begging now, halfway down the center aisle, almost in tears.

I was still immobile, unmoving, not even an inch. I was Lot's wife as they departed Sodom and Gomorrah, frozen with my head bowed and my eyes closed tight.

"Another stanza," the preacher said to the organist, calling forth a hymn. He was running out of time now. The deacons were almost through praying with those who had come forward. The front of the sanctuary was beginning to clear. "Our Father in Heaven, hallowed be thy Name," he prayed. "Bring up the boy," he said, and I knew he meant me. "Compel him forth with your power and mercy, Christ our Lord, God the Father of Abraham and Isaac and Jacob. Get up here before it's too late," he begged.

But still, I didn't move.

The preacher wiped the sweat from his face and brow with a silky white handkerchief, the final note of the hymn resonating in the thick stagnant air. By the time he looked toward the back of the room again, I was gone.

I visited that old church house some time ago, a short time ago from now, but many years later from when I once attended. I drove past the once familiar landscapes, plots of land changed hands many times over now, my favorite roadside cafes and pizzerias now shuttered or bearing different names, and houses now built over ground that once earthed the broadleaf and shade tobacco that has long flourished in the fertile loams of the Connecticut River Valley. I drove down the Main Street where the old Masonic lodge still stands, albeit in a state of disrepair, the pallor of its once white exterior a few shades greyer from the years of road grime and exhaust fumes given off by the thousands of diesel trucks and city buses and passenger cars that have passed by over the years.

The two old maple trees on the front lawn are still there, slightly more gnarled now and perhaps not as tall or as far apart as I had pictured them then with my five-year-old eyes. The short path beaten into the grass between the trees from our many youthful footraces and games of "tag" or "monkey in the middle" on short little legs has now grown over.

I recall it well, my time spent there. And I wouldn't say very fondly. I just recall it. Like catching a glimpse of the back of my neck in the barber's mirror or something. Like a never too distant memory. It is attached to me. I just don't visit it very often. But it is always there, resonating, lingering.

There is a wooden sign for a church posted there now, the lodge's faded façade absent its once prominent squares and compasses of the Freemasonry. I did not catch the religious denomination if there was in fact one listed. But some type of church inhabits it nevertheless, perhaps one not unlike the one that I once attended there some thirty years ago.

The church sign seems out of place there though, its small lettering in stark contrast to the broad signs and symbols that were once so commonplace. What should be there instead is a headstone. A marble marker to commemorate the fallen, with "Here lies my faith" for an epitaph. Or "Herein is where I lost my religion, so many moons ago." Or "Underneath here is the hellfire, through these doors is where the brimstone begins." Or so we were led to believe, looking into the old, cavernous gas furnace for punishment.

I drove past the old front porch steps, slightly canted now, and not quite as steep of a climb as I remembered them. The porch steps where my mother had walked down with my stepdad on their wedding day and all the church members had lined up to toss the proverbial handfuls of rice in their direction. It's where my parents celebrated their marriage, my stepdad's first and my mother's third.

That old lodge was where the summer Vacation Bible School took place and where we sipped cherry Kool-Aid poured from big plastic Igloo containers into paper Dixie cups. It's where we ate our church suppers on the side veranda overlooking the World War I memorial with the bronze doughboy statue standing sentry over the intersection.

"Here lie the remnants of the truth," Truth Baptist Church that is, which is what its name was, the church I once attended at that same place. Truth. That was its name in some ironic twist of fate. In this place born of deceit. Never was a more foreign word spoken.

I got my first job there, at the Masonic lodge. Helping my stepdad and the pastor set up for Sunday morning services. At five or six years old such was my important tasking. Taking down the dusty symbols and banners of the Freemasonry and covering them with the church's own banners inscribed with scripture verses or the Christian flag, moving the ash trays and replacing those with the church's offering plates, neatly folding and stacking the paper bulletins, and passing out the homemade hymnals collated in the pastor's own basement. Sometimes I'd run the vacuum cleaner between the rows of metal folding chairs being careful not to tangle the electrical cord amid the narrow spaces.

"Here lies where it all began," the epitaph might say. "Where one meets God and the corresponding burdens of such a meeting." Or such an inscription might read, "This is where a young and ambitious pastor from the Midwestern prairies was instructed by God to start up a 'fundamentalist Bible-believing' church in a small Connecticut shit town on a wing and a prayer and a few dollars in seed money before he lost his way and his truths became deceits. (P.S. And before he and his congregants would find themselves in the newspapers and on the television news reports and in prisons for crimes committed in Jesus' name. . . .)"

Or perhaps, "Here lie my parents' vows," it might read. Where my mother would leave them some ten years later, dried out and wilted like so many discarded flower petals from the bridal bouquet she had tossed to some poor, hopeful unfortunate in the crowd of single ladies. Or maybe, "Here lie the first scattered shards of the faithful," or "This marks the spot where Santa Claus was no longer . . . and the Easter Bunny was discovered to be a tool of the devil." It could go on and on, this epitaph. A solitary inscription marking an empty lawn inhabited now by the ghosts of Freemasons and a lone soldier's gaze frozen in time across the street by the Raymond Library.

La Fata Morgana

You wanted to fuck your Sunday school teachers at the fundamentalist Baptist church you grew up in long before you knew how. Because you were like ten years old, and because, well, you knew there was something under there that you wanted. Under all those layers of clothes and scarves and dark nylons and tights and non-push-up bras and prim medium heels and "Jesus saves" and "Thou shalt nots"–under all of it, you knew they were keeping something from you, some beautiful secret that you couldn't know yet.

Now you think, was I this depraved at that young age? Maybe. Probably. And both terrified and excited by the prospect of those ladies being something else other than your virtuous Sunday morning teachers with their quiet voices and the joy of Jesus radiating from their unmade-up faces. Actually, that's not entirely accurate. You will always remember the one who wore a hint of purple eyeliner like a secret seventies pinup who would effectively be the ground zero of your lifelong affection for longhaired brunettes with soft brown eyes. She would later be publicly humiliated and cast out for having an extramarital affair–for wanting something more out of life than continual near-poverty, four kids, and not a goddamn thing to look forward to.

Back to Sunday school though, the root of all your lustful evils. Because you are homeschooled and your contact with the outside world was limited to this weekly occurrence, your first experience with sexual desire was with the women of the church congregation. You must have been about eleven or twelve when you first began to notice the soft curves of their calves, their thighs and hips, the fleshy roundness of their haunches, their smooth skin, the lines of their necks and shoulders, the suggestion of a smile on their lips, their delicate eyelashes and their soft looking hair.

You'd find yourself sneaking peeks of them during prayers when your eyes were supposed to be closed and your head was supposed to be bowed, and sometimes they'd catch you, and you'd shut your eyes tight again. When you were younger, you'd feel your face growing red and your ears hot, and you'd try not to sneak peeks for a while; but it's not long before you're doing it again, and a couple of years older, and you're no longer closing your eyes so tight.

Instead, you're holding their gaze for a few seconds longer, or flashing them a shy "Oops, pray for me, I'm caught" smile; and they'd smile back, and for those brief moments you'd be sharing a secret—this illicit thing between only the two of you. Soon you're holding their gazes just a little longer each time, and your face is not growing so red and your ears are not as hot until you don't think twice about doing it.

At first, they may be your Sunday school teacher, or your friend's mother, the deacon's wife, or a visiting missionary lady, the pianist, or some other member of the congregation that you have known as long as you can remember. And later, it will be the wives and teenage daughters of your Sunday school teachers once you have reached the age where your Sunday school classes have become separated by your sex. You will be fourteen or fifteen then, and they will be just home from college, or new mothers in their twenties and thirties, or single divorcées, and you will begin to take note of the subtler signs of attraction and flirtation.

You imagine what they might feel like then: their hair, their fingertips, the softness of their breasts, the taste of their mouths and lips. And how they might smell: their necks of some very sparingly applied perfume maybe, and their just washed hair still slightly damp from the shower. From your seat in the church pew, you watch the way their fingers turn the pages of hymnals and Bibles, and as they adjust their skirts to cross or uncross their legs. As they stand to leave their pews, you notice the way their hips move as they step sideways into the aisle and listen to the quiet rustling of their dresses and the slips underneath, catching the occasional glimpse of pale ankle leading upward towards a calf muscle now taut with the weight of their full height.

You see the way their faces flush in the heat of the summer revival meetings and the sweat as it glistens on their necks and the lines of their clavicles, and how their thin dresses cling to their skin, and how they brush the hair back from their foreheads and make little "O" shapes and blowing sounds with their lips as if they could magically cool everyone off. Like they're blowing out birthday candles, you think. Twenty or thirty even. And it makes your heart beat faster; and because you don't know why, you move from face to face across the aisles estimating their ages in candles. You would blow out birthday candles with them if they wanted you to, you think. They would need help with that many candles. And then they would kiss you with those "O" shaped lips, as your earliest lustful indulgences went.

During the singing of the hymns, you will begin to think that the swell of their breasts, small or full, younger or older, is a thing of wonder and beauty; but not to touch, only to look, and so you will steal glances from time to time only slightly risking eternal damnation. You will not be as fascinated by this, though, as you will be with the swishing of their skirts and dresses as they walk. Perhaps because this is what is at a comfortable eye level for you, being a stepchild and the product of divorced parents—your gaze habitually downcast as the son of the sinful—this is why you can look on uninterrupted and unnoticed. This is what you study. This is what you will look for first in a woman, their legs. These will be your first measure of feminine physical attractiveness.

The female form, the Marilyn Monroe-esque gam, the *Christmas Story* leg lamp, this you will from here on follow blindly, stupidly, like a thirsty Bedouin following a mirage of a glistening pool of water, or the La Fata Morgana-fixated sailor after a sculpted set of towering golden calves. Often, you will have some premonition that chasing after such phenomena will lead to your doom, but you will run after them nevertheless. More often, as you grow older and have become slightly less the man-child, you will feel your ego wrestling with your id in regard to such indulgences, and you may successfully withstand the temptation to be mesmerized by the sharp click of a pair of stilettos on hardwood or tile and the scissored newly confident march of a housewife turned Venus by strappy heels from Bloomingdales—but still, still you will struggle to avert your eyes.

You will accept a ride from an attractive woman one day after your high school soccer practice when you are sixteen and waiting for the city bus because you can see that she is wearing a skirt, and she has tan legs and long curly dark hair and a nice smile and sunglasses, and she is the Monica Bellucci of your earliest fantasies. And you will discover that once you are in the car with her, that she is on her way home from her job, and that her fiancé has just broken up with her, and she will begin crying, and her mascara will run down her face. Soon, you will also learn that she left work early and went to a bar, and that now she is shitfaced and swerving all over the road, and you will beg her to stop the car and let you out because all of a sudden you will not want to die in this car with this terribly upset, beautiful woman. And she will argue with you that she isn't drunk and will berate you for not being *a man*, because she needs *a man*, and you're just a kid, and she will be your first woman scorned—her and her bronzed legs that will stay with you long after you are *a man*.

You will wonder later where she was taking you that day, why you never thought about that before you got in the car with her, what you would have even done if she had brought you home with her. You were still a virgin then and had barely ever sloppily made out with high school girls in the back seats of their parent's cars. And you will continue to be drawn into other women's cars by their nice smiles and their golden legs and their tears and their distress and their hurt and their engagements and their marriages and their careers and your own curiosity and sympathy and loneliness and depression and lust. But mostly because of your lust. You will too soon forget everything else, and only your lust will remain.

You will notice the arches of their feet as they dangle their shoes off their toes in church pews, and in college classrooms, and in corporate conference rooms, and in cubicles across from yours, and you will think about how elongated their legs look in their heels as they walk in them. You will buy them expensive shoes and remember their sizes for birthdays and anniversaries, and stop at sample sales, and walk with them through shops in New York and London and Paris, and get things wrapped in crisp holiday paper by people who wrap things for a living, but this will not be for them so much as it will be for you. And mostly, out of their kindness, or hope, or ignorance, or naiveté, they will try them on for you and pretend that they love them, and only want you to take them home or back to your hotel.

You will not be ashamed of this then. But one day, you will wish that you had not given them such self-indulgent gifts and regret the times that you have disappointed and hurt and left those other women, and will want to apologize to them, but they will have moved on and not looked back. They will be in relationships that you will envy. Or they will live in restored colonials and raised ranches with partners and children and big sloppy dogs of which they will post happy, homey pictures over their social media accounts. They will have good jobs in safe places and stable boyfriends who bring them flowers and don't leave them when the monotony of suburbia pales in comparison to the deserts of North Africa.

They will not miss you or think of you when you are drinking alone in hotel bars in New York, or curled up on your couch with your cat and a bottle of wine watching Ken Burns's *The Vietnam War* and weeping years later. And you will regret this and think about trying to call them or write to them, but you will know they will not reply. You will be forgotten. And you will know that you deserve to be forgotten.

Bedroom Eyes

"**Y**ou have bedroom eyes," she says to you with a little smile. "Bedroom eyes," you repeat, handing her ID card back to her, your fingers touching for a second, and lingering for a second longer. You are looking back into her own eyes, searching her face, guessing at what she means, but not exactly knowing.

"Mm-hmm," she says with a perfectly shaped eyebrow raised. And she laughs a little laugh as she saunters away and looks back at you watching her walk.

"Bedroom eyes," you repeat again.

"Yeah, dude." Your coworker and recently new roommate smirks. He is a Marine, and twenty-seven, infinitely older and wiser than you, and you look to him as the older brother you've never had and always wanted.

"What the hell is that?" you wonder aloud. You think you might know, but you're not 100 percent. He laughs.

"She wants to fuck you, man," he says. And you both snicker at the simplicity of his explanation. It makes perfect sense to you now. Of course, it does.

"That's awesome," you say. But you think, what if she really does though?

He shakes his head. "I swear, you grew up in a cave."

"I really did kind of," you say. "Well, it might as well have been. A Baptist cult is cave enough."

He nods solemnly, and the two of you move on to trying to guess her age. Thirty-five he says. You say thirty-two. But you're not really sure because you're nineteen and this is beyond the scope of your experience. But because the two of you are security guards at a corporate office and sit behind a desk together most of the shift, you have a lot of time to debate such things over coffee and whatever snacks anyone has brought in, while checking IDs and signing in visitors.

You are a little shier the next time she comes by because now you know she's thinking about having her way with you, and so you don't look at her at first until you realize that she's standing there waiting for you to acknowledge her. And when you finally do, she gives you a look that makes your pulse quicken and your face turn a shade of crimson it hasn't since you were a boy. "Hey you," she says. And she says she's going out and asks you if you there's anything she can bring you, and you just smile back at her kind of dumbly until you feel your roommate kick you under the desk, and you manage to say something way less witty than you ever imagined you would.

"Can I bring you . . . *something?*" your roommate mimics after she's gone and gives your shoulder a shove. You give him a shove back and pause to listen as she walks to her car clicking the pavement in her high heels and pencil skirt.

"I'd do it, man," he says.

"Yeah?"

"Definitely." And so now this is all you will think about. The logistics of it. The immorality of it.

Until one afternoon, she's standing at the desk talking to you before she leaves for the day like she normally does, and she asks you if you might like to stop over for a glass of wine after your shift. "I like wine," you tell her. Which is not true in the least. You've never really had wine. A sip of champagne and a beer or two at a wedding maybe. A couple shots of whiskey with some Arkansas farm boys on your Army Basic Training graduation pass. But you've not really ever tried wine. Even during the monthly Baptist communions, they would pass around little plastic cups of grape juice from Sam's Club or wherever they could find the cheapest nonalcoholic blood of Jesus substitute, but your experience with wine was as limited as your experience with women older than eighteen.

You tell your roommate about this latest development when he gets back from his tour around the building, and he nods and grins.

"Bedroom eyes, man," he says with a chuckle. "You gotta do it."

"Yeah, I'm gonna do it," you say. "I'm gonna go over there." And do what though, you wonder. We're going to have a glass of wine and make out, and then go back to her bedroom and have sex, and then see each other in the morning at the security desk, and that'll be that, right? Okay, then, you reassure yourself. That sounds easy enough. That's a good plan. And so, you spend the rest of your night worrying about it.

"Just go over there and see what happens, dude," your roommate says. "Go keep her company. Maybe she's lonely or something." He's tired of listening to you blabber on about adultery and eternal damnation and illegitimate children and vengeful husbands and whatever else you can think of to talk yourself out of going.

"Go have a good time. Don't worry about it." He punches you in the arm in comradeship and orders you to leave. "Go, on. Get outta here, ya big baby. Go bring *her* something."

"Ha-ha, *something*," you say as you're heading out the door, and his exaggerated shrug and grin are words enough for what he already knows is about to transpire.

You call her to tell her you're on your way, and she tells you not to park in the driveway, to just come in because she's left the door unlocked. So, you do a drive-by until you're sure of the right house, and park a few driveways over, and feel like you're definitely doing something you're not supposed to be doing—something criminal. And when you are on the porch step and your fight-or-flight response mechanism is firmly leaning toward flight, you see that the door is open just a crack; and so, you take a deep breath and squelch those stress hormones coursing rapid-fire through your veins, knock softly, and step through the front door into the neatly decorated foyer of the home belonging to the woman who flirts with you at the security desk.

Hearing the door open, she peeks around the corner from the kitchen, smiles her now familiar smile, and greets you with an, "Oh, hello, you." And as she walks over to meet you holding a glass of wine, barefoot in a kimono, you can tell that she's not wearing much or anything under it. She kisses you softly with her mouth open just enough for you to feel the tip of her tongue graze your bottom lip, and you silently cash in the entire capital of every good deed you've ever banked and not used until that moment to prevent yourself from blushing like a thirteen-year-old schoolgirl whose prize heifer just won a beauty pageant at the 4-H Club.

"You're . . . you're so much taller at work. I mean, in your . . . shoes," you point out unnecessarily, as if she wasn't aware of such indisputable truths, to which she just smiles and pulls you toward her to kiss you again. Now, this is a woman you think. An adult woman who's been a wife and mother and businesswoman who knows what she wants and exactly how to get it, it being at the moment, you. She is every woman you have ever fantasized about from your church pew. She is every curve, every smile, every glimpse that you have sneaked a peak at in every Sunday service you have suffered through. She is what is under every dress and every skirt and in every pair of high heels and is right at your fingertips.

"How about that glass of wine?" she says and pours you a glass of white wine from a bottle in the refrigerator into one of those glasses with the large bowls and you have a taste. It's sweet and crisp like a bite of a Gala apple, and you tell her that you like it; and you follow her with your glass to her living room where she sits you down on a sofa in front of a glowing fireplace and flickering candles on the mantel and sits next to you. But not like you sit next to someone you met a few months earlier; like she's known you your whole life, and she's been sitting-with-you-like-this-forever kind of next to you.

She's definitely done this before, you think. You can feel the warmth of her thigh pressed against yours through your jeans and the heat of the fire on your face. And then you begin to suspect that it might be so warm in there for a reason. That either this is what grown women actually do at the end of their day, sip wine in front of the fireplace scantily clad, or that she's going to seduce you right there in her living room because her kids are sleeping upstairs, and she doesn't want to wake them. You hope a little that she might while being equally afraid that she will.

While you're making small talk about what you're going to school for, what you want to be when you grow up, she tells you about moving from Florida and not being used to the cold New England winters. This puts you more at ease as it occurs to you that maybe that's the reason for its being so warm in there; that maybe she's not so much of a seductress and actually is just a little lonely like you've been lonely sometimes. The wine is going down smooth like you've heard good wine described by people who know such things, and you're starting to really like it–the way it tastes, the way it makes you feel, warm and sophisticated.

And after she's refilled your glasses again, you begin to feel her hand on your leg and then on your arm, sometimes giving it a soft squeeze. You watch as she crosses and uncrosses her legs next to you, feel her hand moving from your arm to your shoulder, and she asks if you had ever had a massage. "Oh, of course," you say. And you're thinking about the little back rub machine that the Italian barber loops his hand through and massages your back and shoulders with after your haircut, but then you also think, that's probably not what she's talking about. And its's not.

She's talking about massages without your clothes on. Like with oils and bathrobes and fluffy towels and heated stone type of massages, the kind you go to a spa for when you're a lady of a certain taste and income. Not when you're a nineteen-year-old security guard going to community college on a Connecticut National Guard tuition waiver who shares an apartment with a Marine and thinks that your weekly ten-dollar haircut is pretty damn fancy. Describing her very-different-from-your idea of massages, she lets out her hair and sighs like she just tasted something delicious.

"I could give you one. . . ."

"Yeah, I bet," you say as nonchalantly as you can manage, like exchanging sexy banter with thirtysomething women in their living rooms is just a thing you do all the time.

"I'm serious. I'll give you one, and then you can give me one." And she looks you in the eyes like she's actually asking and not completely in control. You wonder if she can hear your heart palpitating in your chest. She's literally willing you to take your clothes off, you think. Or that she's taking your clothes off with her mind. You are mesmerized by this.

"Just say when," you say, starting to feel the effects of the alcohol in the wine. The firmness of her thigh pressed against yours. Her fingers softly kneading the muscles in your shoulders. The healthy glow of her tan, Sunshine State-kissed face and neck and arms. *She wants to fuck you, man*–you hear your roommate's voice in your head, and you suppress a smile. She really does though. She's about to. You wonder what it will be like to be fucked. To be the one not quite in control of the fucking. You really did grow up in a cave. A puritanical cave somewhere in the forest.

"What are you smiling at?" she says, smiling back at you. She knows though. She knows everything that's happening and about to happen.

Then she stands up in front of you, lets the kimono slip from her shoulders, and begins unbuttoning your shirt from top to bottom—and you look at this woman standing there naked in front of you, all of her with her full breasts and hips and thighs. Her skin is golden and probably just as smooth as it looks, and as you are admiring her, she takes your hands in hers and puts them on each of her breasts and looks at you like prey. And then your shirt is coming off, your jeans are being unbuttoned, she is straddling you, and you can feel her balmy heat as she pushes herself against you and you into her.

This will not be like the massage she was describing. That massage doesn't quite happen just then. This is where she possesses you. This is where she gives you a big, satisfied kiss before leaving for the bathroom and kitchen to refill your wine glasses. This is where you have the thought that she just took what she wanted from you and then walked away. You don't particularly mind this then, but you do wonder later if you should feel a slight bit used.

And then she's back and spreading out a fleece throw over the carpet and laying you down on the floor and telling you to do this and this and not so much of that but more of this until she comes again like you never knew was possible. You've read about such things in your solitary pubescent hours of research at libraries, but you had yet to experience it in person. And it's amazing, and you think that this is thus far your life's highest achievement; and that you will need to remember this and return to this in future such encounters with the opposite sex.

You are ashamed to admit that you never actually could tell before if your teenaged girl partners had an orgasm during sex. You guessed they did, as far as you could tell. You could hear what you thought it was, the heavier breathing, the moans—but this, this you could feel. Everywhere. This was a woman's entire body shuddering, teeth in your shoulder, toes and fingers and muscles clenching. This, this was unmistakably the female orgasm, the apex of feminine desire which you had so long wondered about like some celestial thing of yore. You wonder how you ever lived without this. You wonder if past lovers were simply being polite and not demanding such delights from you as well.

Do this she says. Now this. And she puts your face where she wants it, and you where she wants you, and your soul where it belongs. And the power to do this whenever you are with her or any other woman is now in your hands. You are punch-drunk with your new sexual knowledge. Or just drunk. You will make a promise to yourself that you will only use these powers for good. But you will not. You will use these powers to bolster your delicate ego and to counter your vulnerabilities and insecurities. You will use these powers to offset your depression and your sadness and your anger and your loneliness. You will not be a responsible steward of such powers.

"Mommy?" You hear the small, quivering voice of a sleepy child echoing down from the top of the stairs, the sound of which will haunt your dreams.

"Oh, my god, that's my son," she whispers, "Lie down."

So, you lay with your back against the couch, and you hear the boy's tiny voice again, "Mommy? I can't sleep. I'm thirsty."

"Oh, honey, give me just one second, okay? I'm coming," she tells him and puts her finger on your lips. He's near the top of the stairs. You can hear his little feet pattering, and you're lying on his living room floor with his mother's taste in your mouth and your hand between her thighs. You look into the fireplace and see your reflection in the embers, flickering back at you from hell.

"I'll be right back," she whispers, grazing her fingernails across your chest, and winking at you conspiratorially.

When she returns, her husband is still away in Japan or Russia or Bulgaria, or some place you can't remember or care about, and her kids are in their beds sleeping soundly. You guess that it must be about two or three in the morning, and you are beginning to yawn and trying not to think about having to work again in what is now just a few hours later in the morning. She says to stay over and come to bed with her, and so you do. You climb into the king-sized bed, and she shows you the picture of her mother on the nightstand before curling up beside you and pulling your arms tight around her. And here you will fall asleep with your head on some other man's pillow, entwined with some other man's wife, slick with massage oil and sin and sweat and sex.

You will go to her whenever she is home alone with her kids, or she will come to your apartment, and you will have glasses of wine; and you will do whatever she says and wants whenever she says and wants you to because you cannot stop yourself, and you are already beyond the point of redemption.

You might have loved her if you weren't nineteen years old, and she weren't thirty-six and married, and you weren't thinking about running away to the army in Europe. You didn't though. You mostly just loved that you weren't supposed to do what you did with her.

A 9/11 Story

The 7.62-mm M60 machine gun supports the rifleman in offense and defense. It provides the heavy volume of close and continuous fire the rifleman needs to accomplish his mission. The M60 is used to engage targets beyond the range of individual weapons, with controlled and accurate fire. The long-range, close defensive, and final protective fires delivered by the M60 form an integral part of a unit's defensive fires.

—US Army Field Manual

W e all have a 9/11 story. Mine concerns a particular machine gun, the M60 gas-operated, air-cooled, belt-fed, automatic, light machine gun first introduced in 1957 and not so affectionately called "the pig" by infantry guys in Vietnam for its guttural grunting sound. The M60 light machine gun is an antiquated but reliable weapon. It's seen service in Vietnam, Mogadishu, the Gulf War, and Operation Enduring Freedom, and variations of it still see service today. A military police team's M60 gunner is an entity to himself. In his turret, he must maintain 360-degree security and lines of sight or sectors of fire. He is the military police team's greatest offensive and defensive weapon.

Because military police platoons are often far from bases of operation they must carry enough weapons, fuel, and supplies to subsist independently of the main force. They must work long hours, covering great distances. They must navigate where others cannot. They must be entirely self-reliant. And they must fight or break contact under covering fire and escape and evade direct contact with superior forces. Here is where the M60 gunner earns his MRE wheat snack bread and jalapeno spread. He is the lever in which a stuck squad may be sprung loose of its confines. The M60 must fire flawlessly, without jamming. Its gunner must fire flawlessly. He must recognize his weapon's specific intricacies and quirks, its fondness for cool dry weather and its hesitation in hot desert climates. That gun is the platoon's lifeline. The M60 gunner must shoulder this great responsibility. This honor is all theirs. I was such a gunner.

Before my deployment to Iraq though, I was also a police officer for the Department of Defense on the Naval Submarine Base in Groton, Connecticut. My first day on the job was September 11, 2001. I was sitting half-awake in an introductory physical security class when the planes hit the World Trade Center. The navy training officer flipped the television in the classroom to CNN and the base went into a formal high-security lockdown. F-15 fighter jets conducted flyovers and plumes of smoke billowed high into the air over New York City. Myself and my fellow recruits stayed throughout the day and long into the night.

The following morning, I drove up to Hartford with the departmental training captain to my National Guard unit's armory and signed out as many M60 light machine guns as they would let us cram into the back of our patrol car. From there we drove back down Route 2 past sleepy Connecticut farms and pastures in our unmarked patrol car stacked to its windows with machine guns and all the ammunition we could carry. When traffic got in our way, we merely went around it, emergency lights on, under federal emergency mandates–I guess. I suppose the US Navy had some type of defense-related powers with domain over state military departments, considering the circumstances. Not that any state or municipal police ever tried stopping us though. With F-15 fighter jets screaming overhead on frequent flyovers along the coastline, it's not like our white Chevy Caprice with US Government license plates barreling down the highway would raise too many an eyebrow. Four days later, on my twenty-first birthday, I found myself assigned to the submarine base armory teaching sailors how to disassemble and reassemble these newly acquired M60 light machine guns. Policing would come later. For the moment, I was an M60 gunner.

As a currently enlisted Army National Guardsman, I was one of the only qualified civilian or military machine gunners in the department. Before 9/11, there was little need for both the navy's own security police and civilian police officers to be trained and qualified on such weapons. In these frantic days following the attacks fraught with uncertainty and near panic, the Naval Security Force on base did its best to prepare for whatever onslaught might be still to come. And one of the defensive strategies that emerged was to emplace M60 light machine guns at the end of the piers going out to the submarines currently in port. And to man these new gun emplacements, the navy essentially drafted its own reserve of what it called its "Auxiliary Security Force" sailors composed of various occupations. Soon I would find myself training navy dentists, machinist mates, electricians, and medical staff, radiologists, corpsmen, and phlebotomists in addition to the navy armorers, less familiar with the intricacies of this particular Vietnam-era weapon. It was what I imagined Pearl Harbor must have been like, all hands on a machine gun deck.

What the navy planned on doing with this burgeoning militia of semitrained machine gunners once they were all "qualified" was less clear. As the minimally experienced M60 gunner on my own Army National Guard military police team, I was well aware of the capabilities and limitations of this weapon; and I was fairly certain that it would have no deterring effect on an aircraft or boat intent on ramming or attacking a nuclear submarine. The idea was ludicrous, a salve on the wound of our nation's unpreparedness. A friggin' Band-Aid. With billions of taxpayer dollars in nuclear submarines and equipment floating in Groton's Thames River, one would think there might have been some better contingencies in place, some antiaircraft missiles or higher-caliber machine guns. Then again, who there might have been trusted and competent enough to employ such weapons. I could only lament these things, however. My concerns briefly voiced and subsequently ignored, I did as I was told. I dutifully trained sailors in the armory how to operate and clean the "pig." More than a few of the weapons fell overboard off the end of the pier and had to be recovered by divers, a task more suited to sailors perhaps.

Policing on a navy base is unlike traditional policing for the state or municipalities. Military policing in the garrison environment can be exceptionally tedious, incredibly petty, mind-numbingly boring, and generally more pomp than competence. But with no other prospects, that job was a lifesaver. When my orders arrived for my deployment to Iraq, my colleagues sent me many a care package and news of the departmental shenanigans while I was overseas. I couldn't have been more indebted to them. I had originally wanted to be a police officer, mostly because I needed to be a police officer; because I needed a job to support myself, my pregnant girlfriend, and our soon-to-be-born child, but being a police officer was all I was qualified to do at the time. I was also strongly influenced by the large number of soldiers in my National Guard unit who were police officers or state troopers. Likewise, knowing that policing was the best career that I could hope for at the time, I was truly grateful for the opportunity.

Okay, enough of the bullshit. At the time, yes, I was grateful and I liked the people I worked with, generally. I mostly wanted the job for the reasons I said. But there was also a lust for the badge, and gun, and uniform, and the small bit of authority and control such accessories portray. A need for the confidence and self-assurance that those small shiny bits of metal and steel advertise to the public, a certainty that I had been so long lacking. And on 9/11, on that terrible day for our country—and for those who would soon experience American wrath—I carried that badge and gun and wore that uniform with a righteous anger and a desire for vengeance. An anger that determined that if the base was attacked, I would have happily jumped on an M60 and fired away at whatever or whoever it was that was coming at us on that day. We didn't know what was happening then, about Al Qaeda or bin Laden, or the coming Global War on Terror and the Iraq War to which I would deploy. We all would have surely manned a machine gun stoked by desires for revenge, adrenaline, and bravado, machismo and near-overdose levels of caffeine, and scenes from *Black Hawk Down* and *Saving Private Ryan* in our heads. Or we hoped we would get that chance, us privileged, soft, mostly oblivious sons and daughters of peacetime America used to fighting PlayStation- and Xbox-generated battles.

And when the story started to take shape and the picture of the Muslim extremist began to overshadow that of the Soviet menace we had so long been preparing for war against, we began to fall into the routine of life under arms. The heightened security measures on the submarine base became ordinary. The M60 machine guns on the piers and the M16s haphazardly slung over the shoulders of sailors posted at the gates became part of the scenery passing through. Sailors and civilians, spouses and contractors, and officers and enlisted grew used to the long lines at the inspection areas, the extra time needed for issuing passes, and the additional scrutiny by base police officers checking IDs.

In the weeks after the Towers fell, my military police company was activated for duty at airports throughout Connecticut, which I avoided due to my being a federal police officer. But on the base, I, our training officers, and the small detachment of US Marines assigned there spent long hours on firing ranges qualifying and requalifying sailors, many of whom had never fired any weapon at all throughout their military career. The thought crossed my mind that if sailors were actually required to defend the base with those weapons, there would be friendly-fire deaths of appalling proportions. They were just not ready. None of us were. But whoever, truly, is ever really ready for terrorists of any kind from anywhere?

The Marines and I debated the merits of putting infantry weapons on the piers to counter what would be an attack from the air or water and came up with none. To protect nuclear submarines in the docks from an air attack, the navy needed antiaircraft guns, MANPAD missile systems, and fighter jets ready to be scrambled. We established that whoever's decision it was to borrow light machine guns from the National Guard was either hopelessly misinformed about the capabilities of the M60 or delusional, or both. But then again, it was us who kept on training navy dentists and nurses and boatswain's mates and yeomen on how to fire them. It was us who felt better after every round exploded and its sound ricocheted and echoed across the quiet fields and woods in the early morning hours. It was us who gleefully fired off any remaining ammunition at the end of our shift, dumping round after 7.62mm round harmlessly into berms of sand and earth just because we could—just because it felt vaguely more gratifying than not doing it at all. As if by doing it, our wasting a few thousand more rounds of ammunition, our long days and nights might mean something. While our nation's Special Forces were already in harm's way on horseback navigating the hills and crags and caves and valleys of Afghanistan, we were shooting antiquated, borrowed machine guns into mounds of dirt in some Connecticut tobacco farmer's long-forgotten field.

"Three- to five-round bursts!" we would shout as the next kid would death grip the trigger housing and the weapon would buck and rip off ten more rounds. *Fucking squids*—we would shake our heads as they would do it again and again and never listen no matter how many times we shouted. And then we would help the next machinist's mate or electrician assume the prone firing position, lock the fresh ammunition belt in the feed tray and hanger assembly, watch them rack the firing bolt to the rear and let off another useless stream of lead into the earth berm in front of us. It was a disaster. The sailors firing knew it. The Marines knew it. The department training captain knew it. His assistant knew it. And I knew it. But because we didn't know what else to do at the time, we kept on doing what we were doing. Islamic terrorists crashing our own airplanes into buildings in the financial heart of America. Americans killed en masse on US soil for the first time since the attack on Pearl Harbor. Training sailors and dentists and typists seemed almost an appropriate enough daily use of one's time, at the time. Each gun that went off was another win for our side, it seemed. Another bullet closer to revenge.

It was a time of palpable anger and we wanted blood. We wanted to hit back, lash out at something, fire off some rounds in anger, without having any idea or comprehension of what such anger and that capacity for violence might actually mean for us and for the world, or for anyone. I didn't know how soon I would get my own chance. Less than two years later my National Guard unit, the one the navy borrowed those M60s from, would be patrolling the streets of Baghdad. We would leave those old guns with the navy and bring newer, M249 SAWs with us instead. We would have our war, whether it was directed at Al Qaeda or not. We would have our bloodlust—as much as we wanted of it until we couldn't contemplate why we ever did, why anyone ever would.

GLUTTONY

Neither reply nor pity came from him, but in one stride he clutched at my companions and caught two in his hands like squirming puppies to beat their brains out, spattering the floor. Then he dismembered them, and made his meal, gaping and crunching like a mountain lion—everything: innards, flesh, and marrow bones. We cried aloud, lifting our hands to Zeus, powerless, looking on at this, appalled; but Kyklops went on filling his belly with man flesh and great gulps of whey...

—Homer, *The Odyssey*

With Our Own Feathers

In the words of Byron, *So the struck eagle, stretch'd upon the plain . . . viewed his own feather on the fatal dart . . . that quiver'd in his heart.* No other words ring truer. With our own feathers, do we slay ourselves, the veteran too often thinks now. But this is later in his life. This is when he has lived a while longer, and has seen some more things, and has had some more time to contemplate the things that are killing himself and his comrades in arms.

But back then, when the veteran has just returned home to peacetime life and suburbia, to the things that one must do to live amongst the civilized, and to the responsibilities that one had before and that still await, he must also return to his civilian occupation. And when the veteran goes back to work on the naval submarine base where he is a police officer after being gone for over a year, he will come back to the admiration of his police department, his fellow civilian officers and his supervisors, and the sailors who wonder what war is really like—the war they hope to see themselves, the actual war that someone they know has been to, not the one on CNN.

The veteran does not mind this admiration. He soaks in it. Revels in it even. Though he is only twenty-four, they look at him as if he is a grizzled old soldier. They are respectful and ask solemn things about war and death and killing. They are wide-eyed and have soft faces and come from quiet places in the Midwest and from down South and from small towns and faraway cities, and they are far from their homes and their mothers and they are lonely. The veteran regales the young sailors with stories about the desert, about the Iraqis, about the sweat and the fear and the boredom and the adrenaline. The young sailors look on in deferential awe. They do not know him from before, only what they've heard of him from the others. They have seen the bayonets and Iraqi dinars he sent back to his sergeant and the care packages the department has put together for him. And they clamor to go on patrol with him or stand the gates with him. He has been to war, and they have not.

He does not tell them then what he knows now—that the war was a fraud, a betrayal of American credibility and a squandering of its blood and treasure—that he never killed anyone over there, and maybe returned fire three or four times, and kicked in a door or two, and transported a couple of prisoners here and there, and chased after a phantom sniper once, and that was about it in terms of his seeing any real action.

What he should have told them is that he was patrolling Baghdad with a weapon he had not trained or qualified on and was doubtful as to whether it would ever fire every time he pulled the trigger. What he should have told them is that the Connecticut National Guard sent him and his unit over there under armed, under manned, and without a mission, and that his company was lucky not to have sustained any fatalities. What he should have told them is that who the war didn't take over there, it would start killing back at home almost immediately after their return. And that soldiers he deployed with would keep dying, as if cursed now, on their motorcycles, and in hospitals, and in their own homes, and in other's homes, some by their own hand.

What he should have told them is that a decade later he would look back and wonder if all he did in the war was contribute to an exercise in American hubris, risking life and limb and health and future under false pretenses for the power elite's financial and geopolitical interests. That he would wonder if going over there had mattered at all to anyone at all in his country beside those who had been there and those who had lived through it. That he would wonder if he should have ever been there at all and if the government that had sent him there had been wrong on this one. That there really had not been any weapons of mass destruction and that this war had been one of vengeance, and empire, and not one of necessity. That the coalition he had served with had left Iraq a cesspool of corruption, waste, violence, and destruction that was little better than the country it had been with Saddam Hussein, and that it would be that way long into the future because of it. What he should have told them is that war is no great thing to be a part of for any reason, even for a truly just cause. That it ruins everyone it touches. And that once you have taken part in it, you may ruin everything and everyone you touch too.

But the veteran does not tell them those things that he has not yet fully realized. At the end of his shift, he goes for drinks with enamored sailors and other hangers-on. They are mostly the navy's military police, though some are auxiliaries and are dentists and nurses and paralegals. Some have nothing to do with the police or naval security department and have only just met him as they have passed through the gates on their way to work. They are civilian divorcées who work on base or wives whose husbands are out to sea. They are enlisted and at their first duty station, and they are navy lieutenants and army captains. They apologize for their sparse apartments and their neighbors' houses to which they have emergency keys and for their roommates' messes and their empty refrigerators and offer him shots of the whiskey they keep around for their boyfriends and fiancés.

He tells them about sleeping in Baghdad in the heat under the weight of his body armor and weapons, on rooftops of prisons, in guard towers on the perimeters of Uday Hussein's palace, and on sidewalks outside of police stations. He tells them about the comforting sounds of the Blackhawk and Kiowa helicopters flying overhead and the Abrams tanks and Bradley Fighting Vehicles clattering past his convoys throughout the city. He tells them about the long hours of struggling to keep his eyes open while in the machine-gun turret, of ducking low-hanging electrical wires, of small children running alongside his trucks, and the worries that plagued him, like failing to spot a sniper in a window or an IED buried in the road or concealed in a bag of trash or in the rotting flesh of a dead dog or sheep. And they listen attentively and wide-eyed and keep his glasses full as the drinks keep going down and the stories flow.

In the mornings he sees their faces again at the shift's roll call or at the base gates as they drive through on their way to work, and he mostly ignores them. Though he really is sometimes fond of them, their hope and their innocence, and their adoration. Their freshness, their youth, a thing of which he envies and feels less and less himself, this he knows is only a fleeting glimpse of what he once was and will never be again. But unless they are sliding drinks down the bar in front of him, he has no great need of their presence. They are a reminder of what he has lost and of what he remembers he was like once when he was like them, full of fight, eager for validation, with no thought of the costs or consequences. And even though he has not yet fully comprehended this, it is their ignorance regarding such costs that is his aversion towards them, a reflection of his own naivety of which he is only beginning to understand, and a hint of the shame he should feel in his glorification of the experience of being an occupier in a land not his own for no good reason.

Fumes Of Petrol

In speed we hurl ourselves beyond the body. Our bodies cannot scale the heavens except in a fume of petrol. Bones, blood, flesh, all pressed inward together.

—T. E. Lawrence

The veteran does what many others in his former military police company do when they come home from their war. He buys a motorcycle with what is left of his imminent danger pay after being discharged along with all of the associated equipment and accessories and attire that one might need to fill the unnatural void left by all of the weaponry and gear and uniforms that he has just unburdened himself of. It is a beautiful British Triumph motorcycle, his first one, and he is proud of it. It is shiny and black and chrome and jarringly loud, and it is finicky and delicate and sputters when it is too cold and stalls when it is too hot.

Because he has never learned how to ride a motorcycle, he has it delivered to his driveway and learns how to ride it block by block. At first, he stalls it, falls over with it, gets himself and the fallen beast back up and moving again. He stalls it on the flat, quiet roads, and at the start of hills, and in busy intersections, and pisses off the locals as he holds up traffic and interferes with the hordes of the Sam's Club, and Costco, and Walmart shoppers making their weekly pilgrimages to those places of wholesale and retail worship.

Slowly but steadily, when he finally learns how to keep the thing upright—finally figures out the balance between clutch and accelerator, and the relationship between balance and weight and wind when taking corners—he becomes confident, and he rides to and from anywhere and everywhere. All day every day and long after sundown, as if being on the motorcycle were his only occupation and responsibility and desire. Like it was anchoring him to this Earth, and without it he would drift up and away through sky and stratosphere and ether back to the desert from whence he came. He rides with the wind in his face and the throaty roar of the parallel-twins' earsplitting fury reverberating behind him.

When he is not riding, because he is working, or at school, or because it is raining, then he is in the garage tinkering with the motorcycle, this inanimate thing that gives him such pleasure. He replaces factory parts with custom ones from California, spends hours polishing the gleaming black and chrome, and studying repair manuals to learn more ways of doing his own work. He could, of course, pay to have such work done, but he likes to do his own. He likes the monotony of it. The process of it. Of feeling the tools in his hands and the grease and oil and carbon on his fingers. Of figuring things out on his own terms. And he spends many hours doing this, often late into the night, until finally going to bed and only ever dreaming of getting back on his big, beautiful, British machine to nowhere.

Because the motorcycle is a thing of such beauty and power and is meant to be ridden in the way he knows it prefers, 100 miles per hour—after classes on his way to the local TGI Friday's to have a late-night steak and drinks with friends—becomes a routine travel speed. Though he knows he is riding too fast, the wind is whipping by his head, the fall air is cool, and the cars are fading past in slow motion; he can feel the engine throbbing and his heart pulsing and smell the exhaust fumes burning off, and so he leans into the corners and full-throttles it on the straightaways and feels nothing else in those moments other than his beautiful machine, and his blood coursing fast and hot through his veins. He is alive in these moments—more alive than he has ever been before—more alive than anyone else, and no longer a mere mortal. Rules of the road and laws of motion and gravity apply to him no longer. Here he flies free of any such rules, or norms, or expectations, or pressures, or things suffered by those condemned to the miseries of the compulsory compliant.

He does shots of cheap tequila with his classmates from Peace Studies and debates the Global War on Terror and weapons of mass destruction and Democratic vs. Republican candidates and presidents and Kissinger and Clausewitz and whoever and whatever else they have not yet tired of arguing about. And as regulars who tip well and do not generally offend, the bartenders like them and keep their drinks topped up long past last call. They send over drinks from other regulars, from tipsy housewives out on the town, join in on the deeply philosophical and scholarly deliberations unfolding before them, and usher the stragglers out the door when the registers are cashed out and closed.

At the end of nights like these as he is on his way home, the veteran will sometimes stand up on the front pegs of his motorcycle and scream into the wind because no one can hear him, and it seems like a perfectly fine thing to do in such circumstances, and he does not actually give a flying fuck if anyone actually does hear him. He pushes the bike into the garage and stumbles through the kitchen and lays down in a random place to sleep the restless sleep of every borderline drunk. He curls up on the couch, or on the living room carpet, or in his office, or with the dog and drifts off into the fitful semiconsciousness that too much vodka dictates.

He will later wonder why he had taken such risks then, why he had risked so much for so little, he and other veterans like himself. He has yet to realize, of course, that one day like his hero, T. E. Lawrence, he too will find himself bones, blood, flesh, pressed against the pavement underneath his beautiful machine, skin and muscle singed, brain bruised, bones and cartilage shattered and broken, blood leaking out like from a sieve. But these things one does not realize when one is still immortal. When still young, and when one has survived places where others wish never to go. When one has yet to appreciate the precariousness of the human condition, the fragility of the human body.

In those times, on nights like those out with other young people only on the cusp of their adult lives, with middle age still only a thing on a distant horizon, the veteran does not consider the thoughts that weigh on the minds of those older and wiser. He never thinks of anything of consequence then. Only of more speed and more alcohol, more education and more credentials, more money and more prestige, more houses and more cars. One more mile, and one more drink. One more shift, and one more number on the paycheck. One more roll of the dice, and one more cheap thrill. One more conquest, and one more confirmation. He works too long and sleeps too little. He rides too hard and too fast and to nowhere in particular. He drinks too hard and too fast and to forget.

While studying war and peace and politics at Central Connecticut State University where he is finishing up his undergraduate degree, he unabashedly defends the Iraq War and his own part in it. He lambasts Europe's soft stance on Muslim immigration and argues with his liberal professors and writes polemics in line with Italian journalist Oriana Fallaci and murdered Theo van Gogh, the Dutch filmmaker and writer. He does it to vent his discontentment maybe, partly because he believes in some of it, but mostly because he wants to believe that his being sent there meant something, that there was some meaningful purpose to it. That there was some worthwhile reason for his life being interrupted to join the great global crusade against terror and weapons of mass destruction and brutal Arab dictators like he and the American people had been sold in the original bill of goods.

He does not factor in the millions of Iraqi lives ended or disrupted or inconvenienced after American boots hit their dusty streets, or of those who continued to suffer—the wounded, the sick, and those who will die terrible, sad, and lonely deaths, too often by their own hand. He does not think much of his fellow students who argue for peace in the Middle East and who question American motivations for invading Iraq. He instead argues for Bolton and Wolfowitz and Cheney, grasping for straws with the negligible weight of his veteran status in his voice, and he browbeats the peaceniks back into their seats.

He does not feel any embarrassment for this until he is in Darfur a couple of years later when he can no longer see such things in the same light. He does not see himself in the same light then either. Or his country. Or his entire life. Only the degradation that has permeated it, that he wants to somehow rid himself of. And so, he tries to do this by burying himself in the work there, which is as far from the shame as he can get. Early days and late nights, without the bottle, he labors in self-exile with the fervor of a monk on some of the best work he has ever done. And this he hopes might somehow absolve him.

The Not So Thin Blue Line

You lost something when you were over there, in Baghdad. Something you could not quite, or refused to, put your finger on when you first came home. Returning to work on the submarine base in Groton in the summer of 2004, you could no longer take your responsibilities seriously. Pulling over sailors and civilian contractors for driving ten miles per hour over the speed limit; the petty drug busts; the repetitiousness of driving around in circles for hours; it all felt rather silly. You developed a bit of a superiority complex, an overall apathy for the navy's perception of threat. The best part of the workday became parking your patrol car at a far end of the base and watching the waves lapping at the ends of the old wooden piers. Your shift would be a routine of intermittent college homework, listening to the seagulls, and savoring the river breeze while hoping not to get a radio call. And the void that you felt, whatever it was you felt that was missing, you filled it in drinking at dive bars and chain restaurants later that evening.

Now, take a minute and peer through this window at yourself.

By the time you finish your bachelor's degree two years later, you will be a semifunctioning alcoholic. You will binge drink and pass out on your front lawn, in your car, on your back porch, or in the kitchen with the dog's bed for a pillow. At 3:00 a.m. when your alarm goes off, you will force down a liter of water and three Tylenols, take a cold shower, put on your uniform and spit-shined boots, drive the forty-five minutes south, and report for duty at 5:00 a.m. If you are lucky and are scheduled for a vehicle patrol that day, you will back your cruiser into a wooded area and sleep until calls start coming in or the sun comes up. And on days when you are on gate duty checking ID cards, you will watch with disdain the submarine ensigns, commanders, and captains waiting for you to salute them, but you will not. Instead, you will smirk and wave them through like the undisciplined civilian that they expect you to be, uneducated or practiced in the customs

94

of the military. On the rare occasion when you deem it necessary to correct your insolence, you may capitulate and extend to them an extravagantly sloppy flip of your hand toward your head, at which they will look at you with bewilderment. Or you will purposely direct and execute the crispest of salutes to their enlisted subordinates, and to pretty female hospital lieutenants, or to grizzled old army veterans on their way to buy booze at the Naval Exchange Package Store. The navy brass will know that you know how to salute them. They will know that you are deliberately provoking them, that you are daring them to say something. You will do this because it amuses you maybe. Or because you are bored. Or because you're an arrogant prick who thinks your wartime service somehow far eclipses theirs.

On the eve before the weekend of your college graduation—and on the cusp of being the first and only person in your family then to attain such greatness as a four-year degree—you will go out to celebrate with your classmate from your Peace Studies class, and you will proceed to get hammered on vodka-cranberry cocktails and cheap shots of tequila from the bar at the TGI Friday's you always go to. You will stay there past last call until the bar closes, and despite the fact you can barely stand up straight, you will attempt to point your car in the direction of home and drive. Stopped at a traffic light barely two miles from your house, you will peel out as the light changes from red to green in front of a Manchester police officer parked somewhere alongside the road. He will turn on his patrol car's lights and sirens and come after you as you turn onto Route 83, and you will pull into an Xtra gas station and roll down your window to demand why you're being pulled over.

This will be a mistake. The officer will see that you are extremely and unmistakably intoxicated. He will smell it on your breath and oozing from your pores, hear it in your slurred speech, and see it in your bloodshot eyes. You will hand him your wallet with your driver's license and your police identification and badge and inform him that you have a loaded pistol in the glove compartment that he will then confiscate. He will ask you if you have been drinking, and you will ask him sarcastically what he thinks. He will then order you out of your car, place you in handcuffs, and lock you in the back of his Ford Crown

PATRICK MONDACA

Victoria as he decides what to do with you. As he does this, you will sit there with your hands cuffed behind your back, startlingly, stupid drunk. You will rest your head against the hard-backed, industrial blue vinyl seating and stare bleary-eyed out the rear window up at a crescent moon peeking through a hazy, very early morning sky. Your police uniform will be hanging from the rear passenger side window of your own, now soon-to-be-impounded car.

You will listen as the officer calls his shift sergeant and lieutenant to inform them of this now slightly more complicated traffic stop.

"10-4. . . . He's, uh . . . actually a cop—a fed. Works down in Groton on that submarine base. Got his ID and badge and uniform in the car too."–pause" Yeah, . . . uh-huh. Uh-huh. No, his eyes are barely open. Can barely stand up, let alone walk a straight line."–longer pause "Yeah, 10-4. I'll let him sit a while longer and let him take it."

This isn't good, you will think. You will recall that this department had arrested one of their own police sergeants for the same thing earlier that year, and that the new police chief had drawn a line in the sand on drunk drivers.

You are going to hang for this one, you will conclude. Because you are an outsider. A redheaded stepchild. You're just not one of them, the real police, the cool kids of the badged and gunned. Maybe if you were municipal cop or state trooper you would have had a chance. He might have just dropped you off at home a few minutes up the road. Told you to sleep it off and not do it again. Had a good laugh and met you for a beer at the Main Pub later in the week and clapped you on the back with a hearty, "You'd have done the same for me, brother." The perks of the "thin blue line," and "professional courtesy," and "by the way, thank you for your service." It crosses your mind bitterly that you should have joined the townies or staties instead of the feds. Another in a long list of tactical errors you will wish you might have been given a do-over for.

But alas, the officer will not drop you off at your home two miles up the road. There will be no such professional courtesy. He will administer a field sobriety test in which he will begin by watching to see if your eyes twitch as they try to follow the tip of a penlight that he will move from left to right in front of your face. If your eyes do happen to twitch, or what is referred to as "nystagmus," an involuntary twitch or jerking of the eyes, you will fail this test. People who fail this test, when it is administered by a police officer who suspects you of driving under the influence of alcohol or narcotics, will likely either be under the influence of some substance or suffering from a neurological condition or sleep deprivation. However, if they happen to also smell like vodka, slur their words, and sway as they stand, they are more than likely drunk. And you will not pass this test since you are quite unmistakably and thoroughly intoxicated.

You will also not pass the test where you will attempt to walk heel-to-toe in a straight line for nine steps, turn around, and walk in the same heel-to-toe fashion back to your starting point. You will not be able to come close to anything that resembles a heel-to-toe step or walk in anything close to a straight line for that matter. And you will not bother with the nine steps after your first two are so egregiously executed that you will just stop trying and will instead just shake your head no. He will nod with his lips pursed tight and instruct you to tilt your head back with your eyes closed while attempting to touch the tip of your index finger to your nose. You will not be able to do this with either finger though. Your finger will not remember where your nose is on your face, and your nose will not go out of its way to help you in the least bit, and you will curse the extremities that have betrayed you in this pivotal moment.

The officer will then instruct you to stand on one leg and count to ten by the thousands—one one-thousand, two one-thousand . . . . —an instruction you will snort at and stand on one leg for a near millisecond before wobbling precariously, dropping your raised foot back down, and shaking your head no once again. He will purse his lips even tighter and instruct you to recite your A, B, Cs backwards from Z to A of which you will attempt halfheartedly and get from Z to Y. You have not been able to accomplish any of these tasks in the least bit, and you don't see the point of continuing. You are not getting out of this one. *The pipes have called, Danny boy. Summer's gone, you're getting arrested.* And so, you call it. "Dude . . ." you say to the officer. "I'm done here. I'm wrecked." He will nod in agreement and administer the breathalyzer test before placing you back in handcuffs and returning you to the backseat of the patrol car. You will not pass this test either.

For about an hour, you will drift in and out of sleep in the back of the patrol car, while the officer waits to administer the breathalyzer again. This is his concession to you. He will wait an hour to see if you sober up any before giving you your final reading. But you will not sober up at all. Not even a little. The officer will hold the breathalyzer device up to your mouth again, and you will blow, and your blood alcohol content will be even higher than the first time.

"Holy shit," he will mutter under his breath, and he will sit you back down in the patrol car again. "Yeah, he's higher now," you will hear him say to his lieutenant. "I had him sit for an hour and let him try again, but he's blowing hotter."

Oh yeah, you really are fucked, you will think and silently congratulate yourself for not killing anyone in the process and scoring higher on that last test. Such an overachiever you are. And you will fall asleep again and not wake up until the officer, the shift sergeant, and a lieutenant are pulling you out of the car and pouring you onto a bench in the police department lockup.

"What'd they get you for?" another drunk will ask.

To which you will slur something to the effect of, "What's it looks like fer? I'm flicking three shits to the wand, man." You will be belligerent. And pissy. And annoyed at the police officer and the sergeant and the lieutenant and yourself and the world that's out to get only you for making the stupid decision of being a fed instead of a municipal or state law enforcement officer. You will curl up on the bench and go back to sleep until they wake you to blow again on the breathalyzer machine and have one last shot at a passable reading.

"Okay, you know how to do this," the police officer says. "Last chance, man."

"Yeah, yeah, don't I know it," you will say and blow into the machine—morning breath and the residue of six or eight drinks colliding into the little plastic tube and spiking it right past the legal limit of .08. You will see all three of their heads shake, and you will not care at this point.

"Nope," the officer says, and the lieutenant gives the orders to book you on DUI charges and to impound your car. You will hear him on the phone with the midnight-shift lieutenant from your own department and hear her raspy, cigarette-charred, on-the-verge-of-throat-and-lung-cancer-sounding voice as she gleefully takes down the information. And you will dislike her even more and wish every terminal affliction down upon her.

"Sorry, man," the officer will be apologetic. He will know that he's fucked you. The sergeant and lieutenant will be less apologetic, but they will also know that they've fucked you—betrayed a brother. Or at least a cousin.

"Chief's directive," they will explain. It's you or me, in other words. "Sure, Benedict," you will mutter. "Judases," you will accuse. "Don't bother to come to Groton," you will say, as if they ever would. You will be a self-righteous inebriated fool making empty threats. You will accuse them of hating America and of being ungrateful for you answering your country's call to arms as they cowered in Dunkin Donuts parking lots. You will call them shirkers and malingerers of the worst kind.

It will not occur to you then that something might be very wrong with you. It will be almost 6:00 a.m. The sun will be coming up. It will be the dawn of your reformation.

HUBRIS (PRIDE)

In Greek tragedy, excessive pride towards or defiance of the gods, leading to nemesis; in extended usage, excessive pride or self-confidence.

—The Oxford Dictionary of Phrase and Fable

In Defiance Of The Gods

*D*o it then, you fuck. Fuck you, you think as you lean into the wind and throttle down hard, gunning the bike just feet from the glistening blue Maserati's rear bumper. You are on the Merritt Parkway in Fairfield County, Connecticut, playing 100-mile-per-hour chicken with who you imagine is some trust fund brat and his platinum blonde female companion who cut you off coming off an onramp about twenty miles back. You caught him on one of the corners and flipped him off, and he swerved and slammed his brakes on in front of you and took off again. But instead of letting it go, you passed him on the right with a high-revving scream of the engine and pulled a quick, no-brake downshift, engine-braking rapidly and slowing down the bike with no warning.

In your rearview mirror, you watched as their laughter turned to horror and the woman began shouting and slapping at the guy to slow down. *No pussy for you tonight, motherfucker.* And you waggled a gloved middle finger in the air daring him to come back and go again. He doesn't though. He's had enough. He gets off at the next exit to take his pissed-off girlfriend or wife or other man's wife home and nurse his wounds. Or so you imagine.

You are a little disappointed by this. You would have kept playing. You would have rammed that laughter right back down his fucking throat and watched as it got tangled in his silver spoon and choked him to death on the vomit he spewed all over his soft custom Italian leather interior and her $900 Louboutins. Or waited until you both pulled to the side of the road, and he took a swing at you, and you beat his ass in front of his lady. And then she'd step over him, lying there knocked out in his Brooks Brothers tweed jacket, in one long-legged stilettoed stride and jump on the back of the motorcycle and take off with you, manicured fingers entwined in your belt loops like in some trashy novel. *Ha, silly harlot.* You amuse yourself with this for a few more miles. *Fucking bourgeois Greenwich-ass motherfuckers.* You listen to the comforting, throaty roar of your parallel-twin in your ears and feel the warm afternoon sun on your face and the wind whipping at your hair, and you don't give not one absolute fuck.

There is a hubris to you now. An arrogance and superiority of which you have not felt before. The arrogance of the surviving warrior perhaps. The arrogance of having cheated death maybe. An arrogance in which you will come to believe that you are entitled to that which you know you will not ever return or repay.

You will take risks you would have never taken before. You will push the limits now. You will not care about the consequences. You will take, and you will take. You will bend until things break. You will test until things fail. You will push until things cease to push back. You will not understand why you do this. You will not even consider it. And you will lash out at those things and punish severely when very little or no punishment is due.

You will act as if you are immortal. Or immune. Or exempt. Exempt from the norms and standards and rules by which civilized society exists. There will be a new selfishness to you. A new greed. You will be Icarus wanting more and more altitude and daring the sun to melt your wings. You will be David taking Bathsheba from Uriah, sending him to his death. You will be Odysseus wandering, drunk and stupid and risking his life and the lives of his men. You will lack in purpose. You will lack in conscience.

Hubris will be the bottles of Grey Goose and Ketel One that you will drink and fall asleep with on your kitchen floor with the dog, and in your driveway in your car, and curl up with under an army-issued poncho liner on your back porch when you can't make it up the stairs or find your way back inside the house. Hubris will be the bullet that you accidently fire into your kitchen floor and narrowly miss your foot as you unload your Walther PPK and the racked slide slips out of your grip. Hubris will tempt you to put that same pistol in your mouth and dare you to end it one day when you are alone and sad and listening to depressing music on repeat. Hubris will make out with nineteen-year-old waitresses in the parking lot of 24-hour diners and neglect to remember their names or ever call them again.

Hubris will be the voice in your head a year later that says *go ahead and pull that trigger*, you little shit when a fourteen-year-old kid with a battered AK-47 is pointing it at your chest because you don't care and because you wonder what it would feel like. Except you will not see a teenage African kid staring back at you, you will see yourself— angry and defiant and full of hate and envy and false bravado. Hubris will look at the tip of an RPG-7 being aimed at your face and not feel anything except *fuck you*. Hubris will feel anger when you should feel fear. Hubris will feel vengeance when you should feel guilt. Hubris will feel shame instead of sorrow. Hubris will drive you to the end of your physical and mental limits when you should feel need. Hubris will make you feel hatred when you should feel compassion.

Hubris will push away the loves of your life. The kind, and the giving, the beautiful, and the forgiving, the patient, and the sweet. Instead, hubris will attract the vindictive, and the self-serving, the spiteful, and the self-consumed, the poisonous, and the disloyal. Hubris will find the psychotic and tyrannical. Hubris will betray. Hubris will seduce. Hubris will confuse and frustrate and paralyze the heart and soul until you no longer know yourself. Hubris will mistrust and second-guess. Hubris will be destructive and respond bitingly and with sarcasm and cruelty when you should respond with sympathy.

Hubris will be the inferiority complex that drives you to multiple graduate degrees that you probably don't need or even want so you can pretend to walk on the other side of the tracks. Hubris will be the six Negronis and wine that you will slam at a public outing a decade later in New York City because of your anxiety and your inferiority complex and the lifelong chip on your shoulder, and because you are a semifunctioning alcoholic who finds more comfort in the sweet taste of bourbon than anything else in any social situation.

Hubris will refuse defeat with an iron will and an iron fist and instead of asking for help push you to run farther and faster and longer than you ever have before. Hubris will drive you to the brink of your capacity time and again and for no good reason and teach you nothing good because you will learn nothing good. Hubris will only teach you to mask your pain and your exhaustion and your hurt and your sorrow and to put up impenetrable walls around your emotions and to cut off anything and anyone who has ever wounded or slighted you.

Hubris will find you on the other side of the globe, 6,000 miles from the place of your birth and your home and your family and your friends, because you have grown to hate yourself and your life, and you are desperately seeking redemption, and you don't know where else to find it. Hubris will find you plummeting thousands of feet through the air on a rocky KLM flight over Addis Ababa during a thunderstorm as you siphon Heinekens with UN peacekeepers and are mesmerized by the blue lightning striking the wings of the plane while other passengers scream in terror and luggage falls from the overhead bins.

Hubris will decide that fate is the ultimate decision maker and in regard to one's mortality, fate has already decided where and when and how your life will end. Hubris will not fear death any longer. Hubris will develop a "c'est la vie" type of philosophy for everything. Or "Insha'Allah:" God wills it. Or: "It is what it is." Or: "Fuck it." Hubris will lean into the wind on the curves and not think about the sand or the salt or the morning dew still on the roads. Hubris will lean toward the muzzle of the rifle and not think about the 7.62mm piece of steel and lead at the end of the chamber. Hubris will look on stupidly as IVs are inserted into your veins and morphine and antibiotics are injected into them at various times throughout your life and will wonder what the fucking point of it is anyway.

Do it then, you fuck. Fuck you, Fate, you will find yourself saying. *Pull the motherfucking plug.* Even though you know you don't mean it. Even though you know you really don't want to die at all, and you do feel fear about it, and you really do not want to tempt fate or the gods or God or whatever higher power is in control of the lifespan of mortal souls. And you will feel remorse and regret for ever tempting fate and the gods and God and Mother Earth and everything across the Rainbow Bridge and the pot of gold at the end of it and everything else and everyone you can think of and apologize to.

You will be sorry for disappointing those powers that be and will recount every time you ever stared up at a hospital ceiling for days and nights and hours on end. You will vow never to disappoint them or tempt them ever again, just as you have so many other times after you thought it was the end and a machine gun or rifle or proverbial guillotine or tractor-trailer went off over your head or swung across your neck or swerved across your lane, and you promised to live a good life and do good things and help the poor and defend the weak and those in need of your help—if only, if only you could have another chance at it.

This Cruel Land

No man can live this life and emerge unchanged. He will carry, however faint, the imprint of the desert, the brand which marks the nomad; and he will have within him the yearning to return, weak or insistent according to his nature. For this cruel land can cast a spell which no temperate clime can match.

—Wilfred Thesiger

My work as a humanitarian began on a whim. I had been home for a couple of years after coming home from the war in Iraq and going about the business of trying to adjust to civilian life. I finished a bachelor's degree in political science from a state college and stumbled through the motions of suburbia and family and policing. Finding this was all a bit mind-numbing, I fixated on anything that would offer me an escape. And in the spring of 2007, with Save Darfur signs and Not on Our Watch posters on the front lawns of random houses and churches in town, I had an epiphany: I would go to Darfur. Even though I had never before given the crisis there much thought and I couldn't point to it on a map if my life depended on it, it was the best getaway plan I could come up with.

Having spent the majority of my adult life in military or civilian policing, and with my only hobbies at the time being marathon drinking or taking long, aimless rides on my motorcycle, I was not the typical candidate for an evangelical humanitarian organization to hire as a field security officer in Sudan. And all I would have to do was babysit a few Bible-thumpers doing their penance. How hard could that be? I had run convoys through Baghdad for Christ's sake. It was brilliant. So, when the international staffing recruiter asked me to come down for an interview, I bought a suit off a Macy's rack and drove the fifteen hours through rainstorm and traffic over the Appalachians to see what fate might await me.

"Will you pray with me?" asked the woman in charge of my interview. Oh, hell no, lady. I wasn't expecting that. I really didn't want to. I imagined my creator who was most certainly laughing at the scene unfolding far below. Well played, Jesus. The prodigal son returned to the fold—on bended knee with folded hands and eyes closed tight. If only the fundamentalists back home could see me now. Humbled. Religion is a funny thing, isn't it? It kills and it saves; it condemns and it crucifies; it judges not, and yet it judges more than anything else. We despise it and run away from it, yet somehow it seems to suck us back into its grip. And there I was, having run far and long, and on the verge of running farther—deep in the heartland of American evangelicalism, after so many years, back on bended knee.

I tried desperately to remember how to pray and hoped she didn't expect me to follow her lead. I wanted this job, and I was intent on getting it—intent on getting out of the country even if I had to pray like the Reverend Billy Graham himself at a summer revival meeting.

"Um . . . sure," I stammered. "But, honestly, I'm a little bit out of practice and I'm not sure exactly what to say. It's been a little while . . . since . . . I said any. . . ." My voice trailed off, and she put her hand over mine from across the table, closed her eyes, and started talking to God. About me. She was sitting across from me—holding my hand and praying for me and thanking God for bringing me to their doorstep. I found myself sneaking a peek at her face. She was so sincerely caught up in the moment, and I found it oddly calming.

I wondered if I should ask her, why they wanted to send an ex-soldier, far more heathen than believer, to help God watch over their people in Sudan? And why was there no one else chosen for this particular assignment? Was there none among them like Peter willing to pick up the sword in the garden of Gethsemane? But I never asked. Instead I signed a contract to go live and work in Darfur for a year. I caught a KLM flight out of Bradley International to Schiphol Airport in September 2008. From Amsterdam I flew to Cairo, and then Cairo to Khartoum. And then from Khartoum to Nyala, South Darfur.

When I landed in Nyala, the sun was just cresting over the drab, dust-colored little buildings. Stepping off into the cool early North African air, I listened to a familiar sound—the Adhan—the Muslim call to prayer, its long wail, rising and falling; God or Allah, his Prophet, welcoming me back to the desert. I watched a little warily as the box marked "Dynamite" tumbled onto the carrousel and made lazy circles through the baggage area in Nyala's small airport, and a hundred sets of hands, arms, and elbows jostled and shook it as they lunged for the steady stream of random cartons, boxes, sacks, suitcases and duffle bags that were being unloaded from the Toyota pickup trucks transferring the luggage from the tarmac. Crates of produce, bundles of printer cartridges, computer monitors, hygiene products, toys, and other consumer goods were being unloaded from the belly of the plane. Amongst the explosives and fruit and vegetables, I spotted and grabbed my unmistakably American military-grade, tan, hard-plastic footlocker and moved quickly outside in the event the place happened to go up in a plume of smoke along with everything else surrounding the baggage area. Stepping out of the air-conditioning into a solid wall of dry 110-degree heat, I looked at the drab landscape and suppressed a small smile. Here I am then, back for more fun in the sun.

The evenings were the only time I could be alone to think and to write down my reflections on the day's happenings. Lying in a tent listening to the loose sidewalls flapping in the cool desert breeze, I stared up through the torn ceiling at countless stars clustered against a pitch-black sky. The only other time I remember seeing so many stars was in the Kuwaiti desert on the Iraq border. Lighting up a Benson & Hedges cigarette, I watched the smoke dissipate into the breeze, and tightened up the scarf around my neck. Outside of my tent, I savored the smell of the stew of tomatoes, onions, haricot beans, and sheep liver simmering over the open flame. Fresh pita bread picked up at the local souk was piled in a heap on a dilapidated plastic table.

My mind wandered back to the day's travels, and my body ached from the many hours of bouncing around in the old, rented Land Rover. Ever so briefly, I wondered if I should be back home in Connecticut, grilling hamburgers out in the driveway with a beer. The flurry of meetings with Government of Sudan military, militia leaders, sheiks, and UNAMID officers had become a blur—a never-ending rotation of small dingy glasses of super-sugary brown tea, negotiations, backslapping, and schmoozing. "This is the life in Darfur," my colleagues would say with wry smiles. The monotone of the prayers brought me back to the present. What solitude—under a canopy of a billion stars in the middle of nowhere, I thought. Giving the food a stir, I waited for the final mutterings of the prostrate men on their prayer mats with my notebook dimly illuminated by the orange glow of the cooking coals.

Mealtimes in Darfur were not for the conversational. In a place with such food shortages, meat was a luxury, and the guys on my team were happy to have it. In minutes, our pile of bread would disappear, be replenished, and then disappear again just as fast. Chunks of bread would be scooped into the savory stew and the biggest pieces of meat and fat greedily captured and swallowed quickly from the stainless-steel bowl. Steaming glasses of dark, sugary tea would follow the meal along with a few raucous hours of dominoes before the last of the men would call it a night. The occasional braying donkey and barking dog would be the only thing I would be able to hear above the snores coming from the neighboring huts.

This night, instead of waking up to the cool morning air and the symphony of donkeys, goats, sheep, chickens, roosters, and babies crying, I was abruptly shaken from my slumber by the tukal door being kicked open and the shadow of a man standing over my bed brandishing a dagger. Half-blinded from the flashlight I had instinctively flicked on, he rummaged through the tukal ripping my satellite phone out of its solar charging socket and slicing it from its cable. Snatching the keys to our trucks and momentarily appeased, the thief joined his comrades on the looting spree taking place throughout the camp.

Sanusi, the young camp manager, signaled silently that he wanted to make a break for the Sudanese military outpost and rouse the sleeping soldiers. If he were caught by our attackers, they would probably beat him, but they might also shoot him. I shook my head no, but Sanusi had already half-jumped and half-fallen over the perimeter fence and was in a full-on barefoot sprint.

I have often wondered what Sanusi was thinking in that moment.

Young Sanusi, barely twenty years old, just a hint of an early beard on his face, sprinting in the dark past armed bandits who wouldn't hesitate to shoot him dead. Arms and legs flailing, the soles of his feet cut up by the sharp brambles and rocks scattered along the path to the army checkpoint, he ran because all our lives depended on it. He was just a kid really, scrambling in the dark directly towards a Sudanese army or police patrol who wouldn't hesitate to shoot him if they were in a mood. Was he afraid? Afraid or not, he didn't hesitate. He just ran for it, returning with a platoon of soldiers who stood guard as we packed up the camp, and we were gone by sunrise. Two days later the village erupted and one of our neighboring NGO's staff members was shot dead outside their compound.

It was oven-hot already and only 9:30 in the morning. Not quite Baghdad-hot yet, where the dried sweat from the previous day's patrol molded your uniform into a dank crusted shell and your rubber boot soles stuck to the pavement if you stood in one spot for too long, but it was hot enough to make you think about it for a few seconds. The thing about being exposed to this kind of heat for any extended time is that you eventually forget how hot it really is. Some might say that your body becomes acclimated to it or that your mind simply stops registering the fact that it is draining pints of fluids by the hour. This is, of course, dependent on whether one has access to water, which I did, but thousands did not. How the people of Darfur survive even the natural forces against them is a remarkable testament to the human spirit and its will to live.

The two checkpoints between Nyala and Bulbul were manned by Popular Defense Force soldiers armed with small arms, generally Kalashnikov or Heckler and Koch G-3 assault rifles, wearing forest green uniforms like Government of Sudan forces. They would ask for cigarettes, sometimes water, never money. There seemed to be a standing order that these checkpoints were not permitted to collect the "road tax" from humanitarians. Though I imagine such collections were still occurring with commercial vehicles, lorries hauling goods and passengers where a soldier could easily bring in twenty to thirty

Sudanese pounds per passenger lorry if they were to tax each passenger.

I had learned to keep a few extra packs of Bensons on my dashboard simply to give out to checkpoint guards and national security officers. Having stood many military and police checkpoints myself, I knew first-hand how I had felt about the occupants of vehicles who would drop off cold waters in the summers and hot coffees and donuts in the winter months. I tended to be friendlier to those types, and we all did. These guys in Sudan were no different. Cigarettes and cookies seemed to work well enough, but when things were getting serious, the fastest way to the good side of a Sudanese national security officer was as simple as a Coca-Cola and a Snickers bar.

A shot fired into the air got our attention. The soldier motioned for us to slow down and pull into the checkpoint. He wanted to chat so I stepped out of the vehicle and offered him a cigarette. A few words were exchanged but the only ones I said were the obligatory *Alhamdulillahs* a half dozen or so times. The soldiers liked that. Listening to the Khawaja attempting to speak Arabic made their day.

We halted the trucks in the village of Dogi to confirm our location and ask one of the locals to point out the best road to Umm Al-Qura. I had old coordinates from the UN field atlas plugged into my handheld GPS but these were unconfirmed, and I wanted to be certain before we went any further. Dogi, just across the wadi from where Umm Al-Qura was reported to be, seemed to be an extension of the Arab militia encampment purported to be there, as several young men in various stages of military uniform were seen throughout the village.

Handing out cigarettes, the Bensons & Hedges gold pack favored by most of the locals throughout South Darfur, our driver Hassabo spoke with a couple of men stacking long sacks of charcoal who pointed us towards the track leading to the camp. As we crossed the wadi, I noted the tactical advantage the militiamen would have over any would-be attackers coming from this direction. A natural barrier of deep sand during the dry season and soft mud when conditions were wet, coupled with a high growth of reeds providing cover on the adjacent banks, the wadi would slow any advance from the east, and without air support, anyone stuck in between would be mowed down like fish in a barrel.

I could see, in the distance, several additional armed men and vehicles on a hill overlooking the track we were now on at about 200 meters. Assuming this was the checkpoint, Hassabo eased the lumbering Land Cruiser forward, and focusing on the group of men and guns in the distance, the two of us failed to see the two men partially concealed in the reeds bordering the dirt track to our immediate left.

The crack of a 7.62mm round from a light machine gun fired over the roof of our truck broke the relative silence, bringing us to focus on the two young men now leveling their gun barrels at our faces. "Whoa!" I shouted. Almost swallowing his cigarette, Hassabo buried the brake pedal and the big Toyota ground to a shuddering gravel-grinding halt. We put our hands in the air. "Goddamn it," I muttered under my breath. This just might be the end, I thought. What a weird way to go, barely managing to keep these musings to myself.

One of the men approached us carrying a Chinese or Russian sniper rifle with a mounted scope. He was barely in his teens, I guessed, the wild-haired young Arab in desert camouflage pants, a worn brown T-shirt, and black leather boots. Boots, I had noted, were a rarity amongst fighters in South Darfur. Sudan Liberation Army rebels and even many Government of Sudan soldiers and police almost always wore sandals.

Recognizing us as unarmed humanitarians, the young man waived us on in the direction of the checkpoint on the crest of the small hill where I could now count a dozen or so well-armed men gathered around two pickup trucks outfitted with 12.7mm DShK ("Doshka") heavy machine guns. At the foot of the hill, another fighter armed with an HK G3 assault rifle inspected our vehicles while a second individual manned a light machine gun position covering our every move. To the immediate right of this position, I made a mental note of the large caliber recoilless anti-tank rifle aimed down ominously over the track south to the wadi area.

The militiamen and vehicles bristled with daggers, swords, pistols, Kalashnikov AK-47 and HK G3 assault rifles, sniper rifles with scopes, al-hawn mortar delivery systems, RPG shoulder-fired grenade launchers, light machine guns with bipods, heavy mounted machine guns, and anti-tank weapons. The men's faces covered in camouflage *shemaghs*, bodies attired in various desert or olive drab-colored military uniforms, strapped into load-bearing vests, bandoliers stuffed with cartridge magazines, belts of machine gun ammunition wrapped around waists and draped over shoulders, and intricate leather pouches containing bits of the Koran strung from every neck, bicep, waist belt, and bandolier to ward off incoming bullets.

It is a strange feeling the moment when you realize that if someone wanted to kill you, they just could. And there wouldn't be anything you or anyone else could do about it. That one minute you could be a living, breathing person, and the next a crumpled, steaming pile of carrion rotting in the sun with small animals and birds carrying away your flesh to feed their young—the circle of life and whatnot. In such moments, you look for something to remind you that you're still breathing: Blue sky. The warmth of the sun on your face. The fine dust of the desert landscape making your eyes run. Anything.

A slight man jumped down from the back of one of the Land Cruiser pickup trucks parked in the shade of the scrub on the hill. Wearing desert camouflage shirt and uniform trousers over bright blue track pants, as was the fashion, the man had a bandolier of hand grenades slung over his shoulder, a dagger and pistol in his belt, and an AK-47 rifle in his hands. Through Haroun, a former schoolteacher turned interpreter whom I preferred to accompany me whenever available, the little man introduced himself as the area commander and instructed us to follow his vehicle to the schoolhouse where we would have our meeting.

In two pickup trucks, the commander and his two squads of fighters led us into the Umm Al-Qura interior. At a third checkpoint partially concealed within a small wadi manned by a team of fighters, I observed another pickup truck hidden in the tree line; on its truck bed was mounted a recoilless anti-tank rifle covering this smaller wadi's path south. These men appeared to have been in position for some time as they were drying laundry on bushes. However long they'd been there seemed not to affect their vigilance as one fighter kept his RPG trained on my vehicle the whole time. When we pulled away, the fighter with the RPG gave me a friendly wave as if to say, "no hard feelings . . . just doing my job here, friend." As if a few seconds before he hadn't been prepared to vaporize us where we sat buckled into our seats and go about the rest of his day. I waved back with a stupid grin on my face for a lack of any other better facial expression.

The meeting with the area commander would take place at Umm Al-Qura's school. Set apart from what appeared to be the training grounds, the school area had its own enclosed perimeter with two completed steel-frame classrooms enclosed with a thatched material. Two smaller tukals housed a squad of militia and a schoolteacher. Stretched across part of the yard was a volleyball net, and just outside, two field latrines, which were really just holes dug into the ground with a concrete slab over them featuring cutouts over the open hole, enclosed by shredded blue plastic tarp.

On metal folding chairs in the classroom, Haroun and I took seats across from the area commander and were introduced to the school's headmaster. An aid brought a tray with four bottles of water, although the headmaster offered to send for Pepsi if we preferred. Haroun and I accepted the water while silently wondering about the gesture. We rarely saw native Darfuris with bottled water unless they worked for an NGO. The militiamen were not lacking for much it seemed.

To demonstrate the security of the roads and the patrol capabilities of his men, the area commander suggested we take a drive escorted by his men to the market at Sarma, a village just south of Umm Al-Qura. During the short trip, the militiamen maintained fairly decent convoy discipline. With one vehicle on point, its machine gun forward, my vehicle at the center, and a second vehicle bringing up the rear with its machine gun covering our flank, their patrol style was almost standard operating procedure.

When Haroun and Hassabo stepped away for their afternoon prayers, I walked through the market purchasing some tomatoes, onions, powdered red pepper, salt, and biscuits to supplement our evening meal, and engaging the locals in my limited Arabic. The militiamen, while aware of the foreigner among them, seemed minimally interested in interfering with my stroll. When I returned to the vehicles, I accepted a glass of hot chai from one of the men who had escorted my team from Umm Al-Qura. Another young fighter asked me somewhat shyly for a cigarette Amerki, and so I passed around the reserve pack of Lucky Strike Silvers that I had been rationing. The fighters politely gagged on the bitter cigarettes until I was finished with my own but Bensons, they said, were better.

Returning to Umm Al-Qura, the school headmaster invited my team to stay the night in an empty classroom. The schoolyard also housed a squad of armed fighters in various stages of militia attire who would also spend the night.

The following morning was a cold one. The fighters on guard throughout the night had gone and their replacements now huddled in the sliver of sunlight that was beginning to warm the crest of the hill. Long, World War II-era woolen overcoats now served to shield the lean bodies of the young men acclimated to the deserts of Darfur and Chad. In the distance, I could hear the shouts of men and engines of vehicles cranking to life, gears grinding and exhausts backfiring in the cold morning air.

As we turned the trucks around and headed back east from the school to the small wadi checkpoint towards home, I watched as several groups of men conducted marching exercises and calisthenics in the training area. We passed through the checkpoints and headed northwest on the track to Jebra and Mershing leaving Umm Al-Qura behind us. Umm Al-Qura would no longer be categorized in our minds as merely a village, but as a military installation home to some of the most dangerous and well-armed men in Darfur.

Arriving back at the office in Nyala, I dropped my gear on my desk and grabbed a cold bottle of water out of the mini fridge we had splurged for in our office. Salah and Daud, our logistics assistants, were holding down the fort.

"Welcome, brother. How was it?" Salah asked. As I recounted the story of the shot fired by the militiamen over the vehicle, the two young men from Darfur shook their heads empathetically making "tsk" sounds. Salah, who had long since begun applying the "f-word" to every possible use of his English vocabulary, said, "Fucking militias."

"Fucking militias," I said.

"Fucking Darfur," said Salah.

"Fucking Darfur," said Daud.

"Fucking Darfur," I said.

"*Alhamdulillah*," we all said together. And then we laughed because this was just "the life in Darfur."

Looking back on it now, wretched heat and mostly bad food, late nights and early mornings, long hours and low wages, there was no other place I'd have rather been or work I'd rather have done, both then and now. Amid the chaos, I was at peace. And I have missed it ever since.

Praying

The sun is an army invading from the east. In between the peaks of the minarets, over the crests of the high stucco walls of the neighboring villas and far from the street where the tuktuk drivers begin their queues, I am awakened by the first stabbing shards of light shining through my window. My head aches from late-night consumption of cheap smuggled gin and lack of sleep. I am fraught with the task of forcing myself to go back to Darfur; I am ill, and I am tired, and I need a cigarette. I lie there for a moment as the muezzins begin their call to the faithful, the sound of it rising and falling against the canvas of a quiet morning. As the sun begins its slow rise over the city, I will myself to stand and go up to the rooftop to smoke, and to pray.

Though for me, it's more like being in the room as others pray, with the room being an entire city in the midst of a prayer. I am caught up and absorbed into it. The sound of its cry reaching for the heavens, the feel of it, of touching this conduit between one's soul and one's God makes me almost want to believe again. I close my eyes and let it wash over me, and I am transported to another place, one that I have not been to for some time – a place where I, too, once talked to God, by the sea, back home on the New England coast, where I gathered myself, both before and after my time in the desert.

That was some time ago. I am thirty-six years old now. I was twenty-two when I left for Baghdad as an American soldier, and twenty-seven in Darfur where I went on a self-imposed exile to Sudan on a humanitarian visa, to make some sense of what my life had become. I have seen many betrayals and injustices associated with various people of varying faiths under various gods. I have heard the wails of Muslim mothers clinging to dead sons and daughters. I have seen the disdain of Secret Police as they scrutinized "Jewish" names. I have felt the weight of Christian soldiers as they leaned on me for support, now absent some of their own limbs. I have filed past the countless headstones of the various faithful in Normandy and Arlington. I have seen the mounds of earth covering the nameless dead, both Muslim and Christian, Jew and Gentile.

Yet I have found some solace in the Muslim prayers to God, or more specifically, in listening and observing as others pray. At dawn, in Baghdad, I also awoke to heed the muezzin's song. Not to pray then, not to recite the prayers, prostrate in the sand and stone, but just to listen. In Darfur, out for days in the field traveling between outposts in remote villages, I looked on a bit jealously as my drivers and colleagues assembled themselves as the sun fell before our evening meal. I watched as they washed, rinsing the day's dust from their faces and arms, and their hands and feet; as they removed their shoes, carefully setting them aside and stepping onto the unfurled rolls of woven prayer matts all aligned and facing the east. I stood there listening, their voices rising and falling around me, some louder than others, some barely a whisper, the most knowledgeable among them in front and leading.

One who led them was Ibrahim, my driver. I'd picked him out of the scrum of other potential drivers hanging around the tea tent at our Nyala office because he looked like a pirate. I liked him because he drove like a North African Andretti, on paved road and dirt track alike. I loved him because whether we found ourselves nearly capsized in the swirling waters of a washed-out wadi, on the angry end of an AK-47 rifle, or chased and harassed by bandits, Ibrahim saved our lives with the calm of a Buddhist monk and the discipline of a Samurai. When we were lost, Ibrahim could find our way home as coolly as if we had taken a wrong turn on a Sunday drive in the New England countryside. Countless miles and a thousand cups of chai later, Ibrahim had become my brother, my protector, my advisor, my sensei, and my closest confidant in the field.

Amulets adorned his thick neck and biceps, stuffed with Quranic verses on small bits of paper into leather pouches, worn dark and smooth from sweat and dust, and an eternity of hours of wear and prayer. Ibrahim could pray to God as easily as I could call my office from my satellite phone. He could barely read or write a word of Arabic, English, or any other language. Yet he could talk to me through a translator for hours about the Quran. He'd committed much of it to memory, passage after passage, verse after verse, as his father and his father's father had committed to their memories. Far more than I ever could remember of the Bible, that's for certain. Ibrahim spoke of his holy book as easily as he might discuss the shortcomings of the transportation infrastructure in Sudan or of the migratory patterns of the Arab nomads. He never said too much, or too little. But when he did say things, we all listened.

I found it fascinating that the most educated, in terms of the Quran, need not even be able to read it, need not have any formal schooling to be deemed the most qualified to lead this communication with God. It stood in stark opposition to my Baptist upbringing where the most qualified and esteemed of my peers were products of the local private Christian schools or on their way to Christian colleges. Our pastors were graduates of Christian seminaries and Bible colleges in the southern and western United States, the academic Holy Land of fundamentalist Baptist youth—youth that I first despised for their cruelty, but eventually grew to despise for their small worldview, for their naivety and closed mindedness, and most of all for their treatment of others not of the same faith or upbringing. How easily they turned on one another. How easily and with such maniacal joy did they drape someone in the scarlet robe and deliver them up to Pontius Pilate. How easily did they cast a person aside and judge and condemn, and for so little, if for nothing more than to appease their insatiable desire to underscore their self-righteous superiority to their fellows.

Yet in Darfur, in the most obscure of villages, the simplest and roughest of men, African farmers and rebel fighters and Arab militiamen more learned in soil and millet and war and weaponry than in any religious text, led others, teachers and the more educated, in speaking to their God as they bowed and prayed together. Is that not the way it should be? Is this not why Jesus chose fishermen instead of Pharisees and Centurions?

I could have joined them in prayer, as they often invited me. But I did not, for fear of being a distraction. For fear of putting my faith in an unworthy God again. I said I would pray with them from where

I watched. And I did, in my own way. I pondered this ritualistic connection between God and humanity and thought about what it meant to actually speak to God without any restraint or parameter of a particular religious affiliation. Under the North African night sky when one marvels at being such a small speck of a thing in this vast universe, under this vivid canopy of constellations and falling stars, during such prayers, one cannot help but think about one God, whether Muslim or not, and whether it matters which faith, if any, we lay claim to. Just as when one marvels within the glorious and cavernous halls of the basilicas of Rome, or the splendor of the massive mosques in Casablanca or Rabat, we cannot help but contemplate the presence and the existence of God. And perhaps we do not need to address God directly to be in reach of God. And neither do we need to lay claim to the title of any specific faith to be faithful.

On the rooftop in Khartoum, in between those long drags of Benson & Hedges cigarettes, savoring that first early morning taste of robust Virginia tobacco, watching the smoke dissipate into the air, into the wind, all my fear and hesitation is washed away. There is a serenity here, being alone in the midst of this praying city. A peace. And as I stand there with the faintest rays of the North African sun warming my face, the voices of the muezzins now dwindled to a quiet, I am left to consider the questions associated with God and myself, without judgment or expectation.

The Baptist God is far from me here, just as the Baptist God is far from me when I am walking in Montclair, with my espresso and the newspaper, and I hear the ringing of those first early church bells. God, not the Baptist God, or any specific brand of God, is also far from me here. Yet I am reminded of the fact that a God is present somehow, around me, wherever I am. I am content in what the sound of those church bells means to me as I am the same with the calls to prayer, the salats. And I feel somewhat more gathered. Ready to make my way back to Darfur. Back to the carjackings and militia groups and displaced persons. Back to finish the work I had begun almost a year earlier.

We Are The Hollow Men

We are the hollow men
We are the stuffed men
Leaning together
Headpiece filled with straw. Alas!
Our dried voices, when
We whisper together
Are quiet and meaningless
As wind in dry grass. . . .

—T. S. Eliot, "The Hollow Men"

Four burly Customs and Border Protection Officers are methodically sorting through every part of my luggage in the baggage area at Logan International Airport in Boston. It is September 12, 2008, a full year since I first landed in South Darfur to work as a field security adviser for a humanitarian aid organization. My passport is a Customs officer's fantasy; the day after the anniversary of the 9/11 attacks and the guy surely thinks he caught himself a big fish. Thick with visas from Sudan and Egypt, its pages bearing customs stamps from all over Europe and North Africa—and my luggage a semblance of random first-aid items, maps, handheld radios, zip drives, knives, cartons of duty-free cigarettes, Arabic language documents, scarves, army-issued poncho liners and field mess kits, and various personal hygiene items—my arrival seven years and a day after the 9/11 attacks in the baggage claim area must have raised some eyebrows.

"What are on these?" the men demand, referring to my zip drives. "Where are these pictures from?" as they scroll through the digital images stored on my camera of myself with various Arab militia and rebel groups armed with AK-47s, G3 rifles, and RPG-7s. Each officer takes a turn asking me variations of the same questions regarding my travels, my former employment, and my current and future destinations. I play the game at first, answering everything they ask me politely as they tear through my meticulously packed belongings. Yes, sir. No, sir. Thank you, sir, I say accordingly as one does in such a situation when your presence has become suddenly suspect in your own country, when your fellow citizens now look at you as if you have become something foreign, alien, a potential danger.

I try to find some amusement in the whole scenario. Here I am, an American citizen, veteran of the Iraq war, a former federal police officer, held up in Customs probably by veterans themselves who haven't passed their state police exams and are now destined for careers hemming up Americans who dared venture outside their borders. There is indeed some irony in being profiled as a terrorist by the very guys I had probably once actually served with in the Global War on Terror. There is also a very definite sense of weakness as one is forced to stand detained as wide-eyed, gawking Americans file past. And this only serves to give rise to my anger as I am judged by the obese, poorly dressed, sniffing, hacking, wailing-baby-carrying herds of my fellow citizens as they waddle on to their baggage carousels. I silently loathe them all. *Fuck 'em*, I think as I dismiss the Cracker Barrel-grazers and turn my thoughts back to my own amusement. *Fuck 'em all.*

I have been through Baghdad. I have been through Darfur. I have been shot at. I have been robbed at gunpoint. I have been robbed at knifepoint. Robbed of my belongings. Of my youth. Of my sympathies. I have been through the crucible. I have pressed on where others have given up. I have been to the hard places and done the hard things. I have been successful where others have failed. I am all out of fucks. *You have nothing on me, you doughy, pastry-eating motherfuckers. Where were you when I was staring down the barrel of a Kalashnikov? You've only ever fought your way through a pizza and a case of cheap domestic beer.* I stare daggers back at any passersby and answer defiantly to the Customs officers. They are beneath me too, I have decided. They are all 'roid monkeys, thugs, and hacks.

They most certainly all own tinted-out Chevy pickup trucks with Glock and Punisher skull logo stickers plastered all over the rear windows and bumpers. They only ever buy American, eat routinely at McDonald's, and also likely own at least two assault rifles and three or four handguns, as only the best armchair warriors do. They are all inevitably divorced or their wives or girlfriends or partners have left them on account of their deathly dull personalities. They are all quite literally best friends with their dogs, a choice the dogs couldn't make on their own. An exotic vacation for any of them entails an all-inclusive week on a beach in Florida or Mexico with too-heavy-on-the-Bacardi cocktails surrounded by sun-leathered seniors and trailer-park Barbies. Their civilian wardrobe consists of khaki cargo pants, short-sleeve button-up shirts, tactical boots, and a different pair of Oakley wraparound sunglasses for every day of the week, as if they are always ready to go operational for private military contractors. They all have tattoos depicting the Red, White, and Blue emerging from under torn skin.

I smirk at my musings and lift my chin at the lieutenant, the ranking officer, like we're bros. "Hey, LT, whatcha looking for in there? Did you find anything?" I'm taunting him now. Goading him. It has been an hour, and I'm tired and annoyed. I want to go home and take a real shower and eat some real food and sleep in a real bed. I am growing impatient and spiteful now, and so, keenly aware of my own innocence and increasingly emboldened by my insolence, I decide to push these guys to the edge of their patience and discipline. I am one of them, but I am not one of them. That is to say, I *was* one of them once, but I am no longer. Now, I am an outsider. Now, I am a stranger in their world. Though I understand their jargon and rank structure and what their training and procedures dictate and recognize their different insignias and stripes on their sleeves and shoulders, I am no longer a member of their brotherhood. And for this we shall punish each other.

"Hey, Sergeant, I think you might have missed something there, by that underwear roll," I say with a wink. And the sergeant is thus obligated to pick it up and unroll it and begrudgingly look through it.

"Hey, Sergeant," I say, "Is this the height of your law enforcement career? Picking through Americans' luggage at Logan International? Did you ever think that one day you'd be a glorified security guard that gets to sort through people's dirty underwear trying to find whatever the fuck it is you're looking for in there? Do you lie awake at night wondering how the hell you went wrong?"

The sergeant is not amused. His face grows redder as he looks increasingly like he is imagining himself punching me repeatedly in the face.

"Please don't talk to the sergeant while he is conducting his inspection," the lieutenant gives me a polite enough instruction.

But I just can't help myself now, "Why, LT?" I ask with no subtle amount of snark. "Because he can't do two things at once?"

That finally gets to him, and the sergeant loses his cool. "Keep your mouth shut," he snaps at me as he tries to focus on my pile of tattered, sweat-stained Hard Rock Café T-shirts and once tightly rolled jeans.

I smile sweetly in delight. Success. A small victory is mine. "Whoaaa—okay there, big Sarge." I press on. "Don't get your panties all in a knot. And don't mix up my socks while you're digging around in there like a special-needs kitty in a litter box." The sergeant shakes his head as he is forced to fume in repressed silent rage. He has taken over this search now from his subordinates, and he is intent on finding some damning evidence of my crimes. At least some contraband Cuban cigars, or hashish, ivory, or leopard skins, or some endangered African parrot babies, or something worth this assault on his ego.

The sergeant and lieutenant clearly do not approve of my shit-eating grin as I amuse myself at their expense, and they are probably getting close to their limits. Even though my detention has broken up the monotony of their otherwise mind-numbing shift, my presence there has not been a particularly enjoyable one, and they have found that I have quickly worn out my welcome. I consider this as the four men look at me with intermittent fury, curiosity, and amusement. The two subordinate officers likely know that their sergeant is a bully and their lieutenant a petty tyrant deserving of being knocked down a few pegs, and they are not entirely unopposed to their humiliation. Though, it is *they* against me here in this moment, and *they* must toe the line. I acquiesce and try to convince myself to just be content with almost being home again. But it will be another hour before I am finally permitted to repack the hard-plastic footlocker that held the entirety of my belongings from my year in Darfur. "Sorry, no." I refuse and shake my head on principle. They unpacked it, and they will repack it, or I will sit on the floor in protest like a petulant child until they do.

Wow—I take a deep breath and pause to consider my behavior. Why am I giving these guys grief as they do their jobs? Yes, surely, I am being profiled. I am being subjected to an unnecessary search and violation of my privacy. I am very tan. My hair is wild, and my beard is untrimmed, and I am returning from a sanctioned North African country. Yes, I have served my own country in its time of need, but so have many others who have later offended it, who later turned and bit the hand that gave them great opportunity. And while I have neither offended nor bitten, I have brought on some cause for additional scrutiny. My pride has only been slighted, however, while so many others have had their lives and livelihoods wrenched from them without any pretext other than their appearance, the color of their skin, or the direction in which they pray. Yet no such thing has happened to me here. There has been no illegal search, or seizure, or detainment. At any international airport in the United States, one's Fourth Amendment rights are waived in favor of national security post-9/11, and I voluntarily consented to a search of my luggage, camera, and cell phone, notebooks and journals. There has been no harm done to me.

As the officers struggled to hastily rearrange everything the way I had packed it originally, I reflect on the whole experience from where I just came. A year of memories stuffed back into a desert-tan hard-plastic box. I will soon roll that box home to Connecticut and put it in a corner in the attic, side by side with my olive drab duffel bags still crammed with the desert sand and salt-encrusted uniforms, boots, and gear I dragged with me five years prior from Connecticut to New York, to Kuwait and Baghdad, and to Kuwait, Germany, and Washington D.C. and back. My life will go on as normal even when small inconveniences like this one arise. While I am here annoyed and worried only about arriving late to dinner, I have already forgotten about the thousands of people in Darfur wondering whether they might eat dinner at all. Or if they might be robbed, or raped, or murdered in their sleep that night. I have been too concerned with being momentarily inconvenienced to remember them, as I had promised myself and them that I would.

I silently bow my head and acknowledge my guilt. I *am* them—these officers—and they *are* me. I too have denied others their freedom of movement on petty suspicions and my own ire and unwarranted biases. I too have inconvenienced others unnecessarily with the small authority that carrying a badge and gun and wearing a uniform proffer their wearer. I too have allowed my own insecurities and inferiorities at times to overtake my capacity for civility, kindness, or empathy. Alone, we return to our homes at the end of our day, shed our uniforms, and the accoutrements of our occupations, empty. Our uniforms have become us, and within those only our flesh and bone serve to fill them. Together, our uniform-clad bodies prop each other up, other men of the same emptiness—other hollow men, other stuffed men.

AVARICE (GREED)

What a night for a dance, you know I'm a dancing machine
With a fire in my bones and the sweet taste of kerosene
I get lost in the night so high I don't want to come down
To face the loss of the good thing that I've found

—Kings of Leon, "Revelry"

Shiny Things

Iloved them all. I wanted them all. Tall and blonde, short and brunette, Spanish or Portuguese, Polish and Puerto Rican, Indian or Jamaican, slim and curvy, volleyball player or cheerleader and band geek, glasses or no glasses. Girls, ladies, teachers, students, I was a kid in a candy store who said no to few and yes to most. The year I spent at East Hartford High School was probably the most exciting in my sixteen years of life.

My first paying job, at the Buckland Hills Mall selling men's suits, afforded me more spending money than I'd ever had before, and it gave me time away where I could be around girls my age beyond the ever-watchful eyes of those at home or at church. At a whopping $5.25 an hour, it also taught me how to tie a tie, appreciate a crisp, starched shirt, and measure and fit jackets and shirts by sleeve, neck, and chest, and pants by waist and inseam. By seventeen years old, I was a regular haberdasher with a knack for guessing most suiting measurements by eye and a taste for nicer clothing. I liked wearing clothes that, for once, weren't hand-me-downs. I liked how it made me feel when I was dressed up and when people complimented my appearance. I liked being flirted with and flirting with women visiting or working throughout the mall, particularly the "hot" ones.

Those are the ones I chased. Another, and another, and another. A different one. A sexier one. A smarter one. A leggier one. One who was better dressed or more interesting or funny or innocent or whatever quality captured my fancy that week. And chasing after them lead to other more material pursuits. Nicer watches with metal and leather and glass instead of plastic. Nicer cars with more horsepower and better leather or heated seats or some other extra unnecessary options. And as I acquired those, I discarded or neglected or forgot that which came before.

That is the allure of shiny things though. You always end up wanting shinier things. Newer things. Better things. Other things. The latest and greatest and updated and prettier or younger or more mature or sophisticated or credentialed or monied or better-traveled —more and more and more infinite reasons that you convince yourself are worth your time, effort, pain, and self-destruction. But shiny things are deceiving. Shiny things do not play well for too long. Shiny things do not age well in the long run. I wish I had learned that earlier than I did.

I played on the junior varsity soccer team my only year of high school because athletes had cheerleader girlfriends, and because I was too slight to play football. And the cheerleaders were the "hot" girls, the popular ones, the shiny ones. Later, I would go to a party at one of these popular girl's houses after coming home from Army Basic Training. There, in her parent's absence, she and her group of friends were drinking smuggled beer and cheap liquor and being not much else—that is, shiny, silly, fleeting things that are only ever destined to be that. As I was in much better physical shape and more confident than the year prior, girls who barely acknowledged my existence before suddenly found me interesting. But that was before I knew much about how quickly shiny things could lose their luster. I spent the latter portion of that night holding the party host's long blonde hair out of the toilet as she projectile vomited.

What I should have done then was spent more time with the artsy, smart girl that I knew from my chemistry class, who had a crush on me and who knew me better than most and who looked past my weird upbringing. What I should have done is not let that girl go to the prom with someone else and lose her virginity in the back of a car at a late-night after-party. What I should have done was be as devoted to that girl as she would end up being to me, and romanced that girl and married that girl who I had tons of fun with and who wanted nothing more than my time. What I should have done is love that girl and protect that girl and not regret losing that girl. But these are the things that you know when you are thirty-seven and not seventeen. These are the things that you only learn the hard way.

Army dress uniforms are shiny things too. With its shiny bits of metal and ribbon that indicate nothing more than "I survived Basic

Training," I loved the way it looked, and how it made people look at me, and how it made me feel to wear it. When I first wore it home on my Christmas leave, I wore that uniform to the mall, I wore it to church, I wore it for my girlfriend then, and for my friends who were girls who I had written to while I was away, and their mothers, and my girlfriends later.

But what happens when you take the uniform off—and put the shiny medals away in the closet, and you leave the girl at her house or her apartment, and you come back in twenty years—nothing is as shiny as it once was. You don't fit in that once crisp-fitting uniform anymore, and the hot girl standing in her doorway isn't a girl anymore at all. Now she's a jaded single mother with two kids from two different men, and you're a married former soldier with a brain injury and gray in your hair and a diagnosis of anxiety and depression with a tendency toward risk-taking behavior and substance abuse.

As all shiny things do in the end, they lose their shine. It's inescapable. Eventually that old uniform won't fit and instead just hangs in the closet until one day it is relegated to life in a storage unit above an old Baptist church. The cars become more practical. The teenaged girls will become middle-aged women. Shiny will apply to different things and take on other meanings.

Shiny becomes European vacations and better-quality whiskeys and more expensive bottles of wine at Michelin-starred restaurants. Shiny becomes bracelets and rings and scarves from Tiffany & Co. and Hermès and Burberry for lovers and girlfriends and wives and friends. Shiny becomes private universities with greater name recognition and triple tuition, and English motorcycles with custom parts and expensive leather jackets and imported gloves and higher-rated helmets.

Because of shiny, I will cheat on the lovely high school girlfriend that I first wore that crisp uniform and shiny new medals for, whom I couldn't wait for while she was away at college. Because of shiny, I will fall for and lose and squander and fall for again the next shinier, prettier thing, or woman, or opportunity. Because of shiny, I will chase, and having once acquired, lose interest in just as soon as the next occasion or pursuit presents itself to me.

And I won't learn. Just as soon as one thing loses its shine another will come along and lose its own just as quick. Or maybe it is me. Some form of Attention Deficit Disorder maybe. Or some innate inability to ever be content, or appreciate, or love one thing or person or commit wholeheartedly without one foot already out the door. I wonder if I am damaged, if my growing up in the projects or my father leaving me as a child has hindered my ability to ever stop wanting more or better or shinier. Or if experiencing post-invasion Baghdad and seeing the aftermath of a genocide in Darfur have permanently altered my perception of what is truly good. Or if I unknowingly inhaled too many paint chips in government housing. Or whatever the fuck.

Even though I always know what happens at the end of the story, and that no matter how good or sweet, or funny and beautiful, or sexy and smart, or trustworthy and reliable they seem or are at first, they will inevitably disappoint. Or I will. And wherever I visit will eventually become familiar and nonexotic and will no longer be new or offer unending possibilities for adventure and excitement. I will know this, and be reminded of it repeatedly, and yet press on in my folly, my foolhardy pursuit of the meaningless and shallow and unsubstantial.

I will be stubborn and stupid, and destructive and cruel, and faithless and doomed, and terrible and jealous, and punch-drunk and self-loathing. I will fantasize about blowing my brains out with a shiny pistol or slicing my wrists with a shiny blade when one day I have myself become the shiny thing that has lost its luster. I will regret all those once shiny things and everyone I have discarded and disappointed and hurt and neglected to recognize or acknowledge their true value and goodness and beauty. My heart will ache, and I will feel empty and worthless, and my life will lack meaning and purpose, and I will feel deserving of these things.

In the end, those shiny things that I once thought were so important and that were so beckoning will not be. In the end, it will take me becoming one of those shiny things to realize the inevitable decline of shiny things. In the end, the shiny and lustrous person I once imagined myself to be will no longer be, and I will be equally battered and scarred and wounded by life and as easily turned to dust as all shiny things eventually are. It will take me a lifetime to learn this, that there is always a shinier thing. And that if you take for granted those who forgive your duller aspects when you are no longer as shiny, they, too, will find their way to a shinier thing.

Calypso

Without girls like you
There's no nightlife
All those men just go home to their wives

Don't be mad at me
'Cause your pushing thirty
And your old tricks no longer work
You should have known from the jump
That you always get dumped
So dust off your fuck me pumps

Amy Winehouse, "Fuck Me Pumps"

Calypso–there have been a few. This one would be the most like her. Calypso, the temptress. The enchantress. Possessor of lost men. You met this one at New York University where you were both grad students. She first caught your eye as you talked about working in Africa, and you noticed her soft-looking lips and her smooth legs and her long blonde hair when she asked you a question. Later, she would move her desk close to yours, and the two of you would volunteer for the same group projects and flirt and not pay attention to much else. And then you were walking to the subways together after class, and going to beer gardens, and hotel bars, and skipping school for some cozy corner to drink and make out in before your trains home. Soon you were driving her to her apartment in Queens, and sleeping over, and spending weekends with her at your own apartment in Ossining.

On paper, it looked better than it was. You had some oddly coincidental things in common. You were both prior military with humanitarian experience in conflict areas. It might have been a close fit, one you had high hopes for. She seemed like the one you'd been holding out for. The one who would understand you, traipse the stranger parts of the world with you. Except, it was not so picture-perfect when she soon became the impatient lover wanting a more defined relationship. She began pushing you to make your separation with your wife final. To move in with her and file for divorce and one day go back overseas together. You did consider it, the pros and cons of it. She was addicting. She was unbridled lust. She was a cold-war spy transported to the modern era. She spoke semifluent Russian in which she would whisper things in your ears post coitus. She was fantasy. She was wantonness. You also had visions of her stabbing you to death though if she didn't get her way. It was in her eyes, something disconcerting. And yet you were captivated by her. Couldn't get enough of her—of her scent and her sex, her eyes and her smile, the way she said your name like no one else ever had.

After a night of dancing in an East Village nightclub on her birthday, as she slowly licked the frosting off the ten-inch chef's knife that she had used to cut her cake with from hilt to point, you had distinct visions of Glenn Close in *Fatal Attraction*. She scared you a little. But you were also drawn to her. There was a kind of danger about her, something forbidden. You wondered if this was the one you deserved from the beginning, a psycho-goddess. You would buy her a pair of expensive stilettos from a sample sale in Chelsea on Valentine's Day because you thought she might like them. But mostly you bought them because you wanted to fuck her in them after taking her to dinner that night. And when you did—against the wall and against her bed—she had accused you of treating her like a whore, mascaraed eyes flashing, skirt around her hips, bright fuchsia lipstick smeared. And you might have pretended a little that she was. That maybe if you thought of her this way, it was easier to keep things sorted out in your own mind. She was, after all, only ever meant to be a temporary distraction, a salve on the still raw wound of the implosion of your marriage.

She should have known the type, you said: the discontented, maladjusted, fueled by angst and inferiority and frustration and barely propped up by alcohol and cigarettes tattooed former soldier variety. After all she had spent many an evening with you lamenting that very kind. She said they had messed her up. You said something about liking "dinged-up" people. "People with a story," you said. "People with scars." She said she wasn't looking for a relationship because she had just gotten out of a bad one. You weren't looking for one either, you said; you were still getting out of one.

It had all been too easy. You had both said all of the right things in the right ways at the right times. You had both given each other all of the right looks and all of the right caresses in the right places. You had stumbled into each other at exactly the right moment in both of your lives; when you were both vulnerable, and wanting, and desperate for intimacy and passion and connection. And after stumbling elsewhere, you both fell hard for each other—too fast. As fast as you let yourselves fall, too hard and too fast. Right off the ledge of reason. Off the edge of sanity. What you both didn't see then, was that by falling into each other, you were really falling over yourselves. Looking into each other's eyes, you should have seen your own reflections. You *were* each other. You were aware of what you both knew might occur, the hurt that you both knew yourselves capable of inflicting on each other and the falsity that you were also somehow immune. You were both self-absorbed, easily slighted, arrogant, caustic assholes hell-bent on your own achievement regardless of the cost. It was Calypso and Odysseus redux, a ticking time bomb of a disaster waiting to happen. But somehow lulled by each other, by yourselves, you ignored all the warnings.

It ended as hard and fast as it began. She told you she was applying for a job overseas again, that you should go with her, and the two of you would live like happy humanitarians over in Africa like Bono and Angelina Jolie, and it would be *grrrrreat*—as she liked to say—emphasizing the "t." You said you didn't want to go. That she should go, and she could just email you when she got there. That, in fact, you didn't want to see her anymore. You figured it was better to just rip the Band-Aid off and tell her. It wasn't her, it was you, you said. That old cliché, yes, but it really was. It really was you. You really were a mess, and you really did want her to find what she was looking for wherever she was going, and you really did think she would be better off doing it without you. You really did wish her nothing but the best, and you really did hope she might forgive you one day. You really did believe that she would do great things on her own and find that special person who would appreciate everything about her that you didn't when you should have.

She will send you an email some months later, from Liberia, or South Sudan, or Kenya or one of the other places she had gone. Something about how she had gone to a party, and Adele was playing—the Adele that you both had reminisced about listening to during tough times and with each other—and she had thought of you. And you had missed her a little and hoped she was doing okay, and that would be all you would hear or see of her for another year or so. You will have moved on with your life and graduated from that university program, and she will not very often cross your mind or invade your thoughts on those lonelier nights.

Until one afternoon when you are leaving work, you will be walking out of Chelsea Market with your colleague, a not so dissimilar long-legged blonde, and you will pause at the crosswalk on Ninth Avenue and Sixteenth Street and feel someone brush your shoulder. And it will be *her*. It will be her, your globetrotting former lover scorned, and she will be smiling that stop-you-in-your-tracks glorious smile and tilting her head a little curiously at the other blonde young woman whom you are now talking and laughing with. And you will run. Well, not literally, but you will step off the sidewalk quickly and propel your colleague to walk as quickly as she can in her heels across the street and into the parking garage where your car is.

"Who the hell was that?" she will ask you. And you will explain, and the two of you will discuss the odds of running into that one particular person you never thought you would see again in a city of almost twenty million other persons. You will wonder if your one particular person had gone there hoping to run into you. Or if she had gone there knowing the time you left work having met you there so many times herself. You will contemplate whether you are a terrible person, because maybe she really had loved you, and you had pushed her away—pushed her away like you had pushed away anyone else when they'd come too close to cutting through the layers of emotional armor you had long insulated yourself with. You will come home that night alone to your cold apartment and your whiskey and soak in your bathtub and think about her for the first time in a long time. You will lay there until you are warm and relaxed and fall asleep with your own lips tasting of Jameson like hers did, and the presence of her fingertips brushing against your shoulder.

The Wine-Dark Sea

You have an entire windowsill of empty Jameson whiskey bottles. Well, almost an entire windowsill. You only need like two more bottles to complete the collection, but that will not be hard to do. You estimate that, in next week or so, the sill will be full without wondering if there's anything at all wrong with this. In your Spartan apartment in Ossining, New York, in what used to be the maid's quarters above the main house, your empty bottles make fine enough décor. You like the way the sun shines through them in the mornings and tints everything under them a green hue. As you are working on your master's thesis in your bathtub one night, you will discover that you can float a half-full whiskey glass and slouch down enough to take a sip without having to pick up the glass. You think that this is a skill which you should be proud of, a discovery you should tell your friends about, a fun future party trick maybe. Of course, you think this when you're inebriated, which is most of the time.

On another similarly whiskey-soaked occasion one late summer evening, you will be on a hotel rooftop bar in the Meatpacking District with five women on a bachelorette party weekend from California. Three of the women will be beautiful Indian American sisters, who along with yourself and your coworker, will be ordering rounds of $18 cocktails like millionaires. Later you will find that the youngest sister, the snarky, sarcastic one, will be the one that lingers, who invades your thoughts—on that night and on many nights after. You will drunk-dial and drunk-text her while you are at other bars with other women, and from trains on your way home, and from your bed when you finally stumble back to your apartment at 4:00 a.m. You will lament her as the one that got away to your former roommate sitting on the hood of your car outside of another bar on other nights debating life and love.

But on this first night, while you are still on the hotel rooftop, you will be intrigued only by her, and you will think she is likewise interested in you. And under that machete-sharp wit and dead-eyed gaze, she will have a softness to her that you didn't expect. It will be her birthday, and she will cry, and you will wonder if it was something you said and apologize. But she will smile her sad smile and assure you that it was not anything that you said. She will tell you about her father dying a year earlier around this same time, and that her birthdays will forever make her sad now. And you will find yourself wanting to shield her from the things that make her have the sad smile that she sometimes has.

The following morning, she will meet you for coffee outside of your office in Chelsea Market, and she will buy you a cappuccino and say wryly, "Don't say I never gave you anything." And you will smile back at her and imagine sipping your cappuccinos with each other in the mornings in New York City and California and Paris and Mumbai and all the places you will surely explore together. And you will thank her for coming to see you again, and wish her safe travels back home, and start making plans to somehow go to the Bay Area for any reason to see her. You will be smitten with this California schoolteacher, and you will barely know her.

As the days pass, and she is back home, and you are alone in your apartment with your whiskey and your textbooks, you will write to her, bare your soul to her, and entrust your delicate ego to her. You will tell her about your strange childhood, and your life now, and the things that also make you sad. You will believe that she understands you somehow, and you will project onto her all your ideas of romantic love, and that she will make up for every other failed relationship you've ever been in. You will fantasize about long walks and intimate conversations in vineyards in Napa and Tuscany and fancy dinners and parties with friends. You will, maybe for once in your life, contemplate romantic marriage proposals and a small wedding by the New England sea, followed by a big Bollywood wedding on the West Coast. You will think about the children that you will have together, the smart, razor-witted, equally sensitive and introspective, and worldly dreamers who will be the best of you both. And you will love them, the idea of them, and her and you together in your It's a Beautiful *It's a Wonderful Life*-*Modern Family* remake.

But she will not believe the same. And she will resist your achingly amorous overtures and your insinuations and your flirtations. She will frustrate your every effort, counter your every overture, and shut down all attempts at endearing yourself to her. You will decide that she has a boyfriend, or that she's into women, or that she just doesn't like you because you are terrible and not good enough for her. And in your arrogance and anger, you will tell yourself that she doesn't deserve you, and you will lash out at her in your texts and in your messages, and you will vow to push her from your mind and your heart. You will swear to move on, and as quickly as possible, and you will relegate her to the deepest recesses of your memory.

But she will not stay there. The best you can do will be to try not to think about her. You will bury yourself in your work and in your studies and in your alcohol. You will feel ashamed of your opening up to her and tearing down the walls which you had so long ago built up. You will loath yourself for your weakness, and feel shame for your vulnerability, and for your frustration and your anger and your arrogance. The weeks will go by. The months will go by. The years will go by. And on those hazy late nights sipping whiskey in your bathtub or on your porch and around the world, you will still contemplate why she has struck you this way. Why she has felled you—you, giant of your own making, iron-willed kid from low-income housing, wanting everything and stopping at nothing—this well-to-do California girl, so enveloped in her family and her friends and her dogs and comfortable life, and so far from you and so different from anything you are or have ever been.

You will think of all the reasons why you would never fit into her life: 1) Because you are a mess. 2) Because she is not, and it would be a shame to inflict yourself on her. 3) Because her friends will probably think you are a savage. 4) Because your friends will think she is bourgeois. 5) Because you probably are a savage, and she will try to tame you as any sane woman would. And you know that all these reasons are bad ones, and they don't make you feel any better at all, but they do pass the time when you feel like torturing yourself. They do make you forget your loneliness for a minute. And as you refill your whiskey glass and light another cigarette and blow the smoke up at the stars into the cool night breeze, you will wonder what she's doing right then, and you will miss her all over again.

Years later, after you have finally become friends, when she has taught you what "no" means, that you can actually be friends and not at all lovers, you will finally accept her refusal as not a complete rejection of you as a person. You will ask her about those terrible messages you sent her one day as you are writing this, and she will assure you with her everlasting graciousness that she only ever saw the sadness in them. And you will tell her that she is being too kind because she really is. Because she forgave you for your arrogance and your stupidity and your drunkenness and your lashing out. And you will love her for this. For her friendship and her kindness and her forgiveness—for being that sensitive soul who cries for her father on her birthday and who loves dogs—and who senses the sadness in other wounded souls.

ENVY

He was a gladiator, though. That makes them Hyacinthus; That's why she preferred him to children and country, Husband and sister. They love the steel.

—Juvenal, The Satires

Among The Rich Civilians

In *The Odyssey*, Athena is a goddess of wisdom and warriors. In this iteration, she is almost the same—collector of wounded men, confidante, enabler. He liked the way her eyes crinkled at the corners when she smiled and laughed as she danced in her new Jimmy Choo heels at Harrods and clapped her hands in delight at the meat pies in Oxford. She was classy and silly and smart and lovely, and he was drawn to her. He was poised and worldly and ambitious and made her laugh, and she was intrigued by him.

One evening back in New York, she called him with her voice full of righteous indignation. He was not there the other night, she said. There was some *other* person there, someone she has only seen glimpses of before, but never in his full-on inebriated and insecure form. The veteran among the rich civilians, an Odysseus for this era, the Negroni-swilling, pill-popping edition.

She had invited him to attend a reading of her latest book and to stay for the dinner that had been planned by her friends and colleagues. And because he was flattered by this invitation and imagined being in the company of such people, he happily accepted. On his way there though, he had stopped at the Carlyle Hotel's Bemelmans Bar for a Manhattan, which caused him to arrive for her reading ten minutes late, a thing that did not go unnoticed from her vantage point behind the podium.

From his seat in the back of the crowded room, he had watched her and the Upper East Side audience as it listened and applauded her emphatically. And feeling quite out of place, he had tried to take comfort in envisioning her in and out of her expensive Prada dresses in her kitchen and in her bed and in luxurious bubble baths and not there in the midst of her enraptured listeners. And though he tried, he could not put the thought out of his head that he might be just another privileged gladiator visited by a well-heeled lady for her momentary gratification–a fascination. A passing entertainment.

On the phone, she chastised him. "You know, you don't need to drink like that. No one else at the table was, and there you are, five drinks in, rambling on about Campari."

And that triggered him.

"I'm sorry I embarrassed you in front of your bourgeois friends. Clearly you can't take me anywhere and are far outside my league. I am a mere visitor to your world, an intruder," he retorted indignantly, his words sharp like daggers.

"Are you drinking now?" she asked him incredulously.

"So, what if I am," he fired back. "Do I need to ask your permission now, your highness? Please don't worry. I won't disrupt your fancy circle of delicate friends again," he said stingingly. His words were too harsh, too cutting. A lump rose in his throat that he could not swallow. And now she was crying.

"Why are you hurting me right now?" She pleaded, "Stop hurting me right now. This is so destructive, and you act as if you just want to throw us away."

"I was a soldier," he retorted. "A savage. A fucking blackguard. I apologize if I don't quite measure up to the standard of your fancy city socialites. Maybe you can give me some lessons on how to hold my salad fork and pick the right wineglass while you're at it."

He was so foolishly, nonsensically angry as she was pleading with him. His anger was fading to embarrassment, and it occurred to him that there was indeed something very wrong with him. That maybe he really *was* a savage, forever destined to be the simple soldier. That he *was* beneath her, and it was then when he could feel it all slipping, spinning away out of his grasp.

"You know you have this thing that you sometimes do," she continued, "That you sometimes do when you feel slighted by people, or by me, that you throw in our faces, about how you were a soldier, and you went to Sudan, in a *what the hell have you ever done* kind of way. It's this dialogue you have, that you fall back on, and no one can ever compete with that. And it's so . . . off-putting."

"And so, what if I do? It's the truth is it not?" he demanded only semidefiantly.

"What you are doing is holding it against me and my 'fancy' friends that we haven't had these same experiences and inferring that we are lesser because of it—because we haven't survived what you have, and because we don't drink as much as you do. This is the narrative you fall back on. I can't compete with the horrible places you've been, or the experiences you have had. You have to stop this," she implored. "It's destructive . . . to me, to us. . . ."

Her voice trailed off, and through the phone he could picture her tears falling, her pink glasses off and resting against a barre-toned thigh or twisting between delicate fingers. And with those tears, he could envision himself falling Icarus-like, plummeting into an unforgiving sea. He had flown too close. Another mortal dragged under in a snarl of melted wax and waterlogged feathers where his lungs would fill with saltwater, and he would black out and sink until he was no more. He will not sink quite then, literally speaking, of course. But something will be gone from him after, from them. Their words, true or not, cut too deep. The void between them, insurmountable and unavoidable, was too far. It was always too far, and he should have known that sooner than he did.

In the allegorical sense, what will die then will be any thought of his ever stepping foot in her world. This will be less of a death of one's hope though, and more an inevitable realization of one's utter foolishness to begin with. When we think of Icarus, falling, wings in disrepair, forces beyond his control pushing him from his lofty heights back to his place, it's *silly Icarus, he ought to have known better.* We rarely wonder what might have been going through *his* mind though. Surely there might have been some regret, some self-loathing at his stupidity, his arrogance, the lunacy of his believing he might defy the odds, that he might as a mere mortal have a place among the celestial.

Or maybe there wasn't any of that. Maybe Icarus drowned with a hint of a smile on his face, content in knowing that he had indeed flown for a little while at least. Or maybe Icarus didn't drown. Maybe he hit that water hard enough to slap some sense back into him, and he mustered up the strength to drag himself, waterlogged, bruised, and thereby humbled, back onto an island called Reality. Maybe Icarus paused for a moment to watch as the waves lapped against the remnants of the wings at his feet and as each feather was gently plucked from its entanglement and freed to drift at its leisure. And maybe that was the last of it, of his lunatic adventure with the sun. Maybe then, that was the moment of clarity.

Perhaps, waiting until every last feather was taken by the current, he turned to embark on a different path with a new energy, his gaze ever forward and all the more determined. Perhaps, while on this path, he is occasionally reminded of the sun in all of its brilliance and beauty and warmth, and he almost feels a twinge of sadness or regret. But now he is wiser, and now he remembers the sting of the impact, the darkness of the depths, his struggle to Reality, and how in the end every fiber of his mortal being just wanted to be back on land. Now he knows how the sun can be when you get too close. Now he knows to remind himself of such things if ever he is tempted to let himself believe otherwise.

What Is It About Us Men

We are four of us, hurtling down the winding country roads of Whitchurch in Shropshire, Wales, in our rented car on our way to our morning classes. Past herds of cows and sheep, and rows of sleepy houses accented with Land Rovers parked in driveways, cyclists pedaling to work, and harried mothers with small children walking to school, we ride.

For the most part, we are quiet men not given to gratuitous chatter, our conversations only as necessary as our experiences and professions have allowed. But there is one thing we can all agree on and look forward to together, and that is Amy. Amy in the mornings. And Amy in the afternoons.

The throaty notes of Amy Winehouse singing her blues break our silence. Our thoughts, wherever they in each of us may be, become infused with Amy's music. With her angst. With her fury. And with her passion. It is something we can all identify with and carry with us along with our own like feelings. Whatever our minds may be, for this brief hiatus, in the car with Amy, we are introspective, our thoughts only our own. We are within ourselves.

If only during the brief trip to the estate where our training is held each day, we are transported to a place where all seems peaceful. To a place where our hearts swell once more with yearning, a nostalgia for another time maybe. Simpler times, when love was something that we could feel and touch, and less a thing of the imagination.

We are men of the world, all soldiers once, from different origins and places. We are a former French Foreign Legionnaire, a Pakistani Army major, a US Army military police sergeant, and a US Army infantryman, a microcosm of our generation's armed conflicts. We are men who have fought and lived hard, and loved long and from great distances, and have won and lost much. And for this, Amy speaks to a part of us long cocooned deep within and shielded from public view.

Because we have all wanted an Amy to fight for, for an Amy to fight for us. For there to be a reason why we've done the things we've done. To be the man who inspires an Amy to feel such feelings for. To rouse such fierceness and wanting by an Amy. Perhaps we wonder if we ever shall be, and that is why we remain so transfixed by her songs. Amy, our present-day Epione. For us who have seen the darkness, Amy is sometimes the light.

Our instructor in these courses, a former British SAS paratrooper who has also been to "the black," as Amy calls it, talks to us of the great divide we are to bridge now. Of how we are technicians attempting to cross over to the world of executive decision makers and titans of corporate industry. He knows the darkness too, and his teaching style is one of tough love for us, for former soldiers trying to make their way against an unfamiliar tide. He barks and stomps his feet and slams books on the floor when our minds wander. And mine is on Amy, on her darkness and on mine.

There is the darkness, but there is also the light. The light that Amy gives us in her music and in her beauty. The light that is within us when we hear the soothing notes of her voice when we're having a tough day. Or after a particularly jarring or terrifying ride through Tripoli. Or stuck in traffic in Manhattan where the congestion is, at times, too reminiscent of the markets in Baghdad. Or in the bustling cafes of Karachi. Or Kabul.

What is the root of it, I wonder? We are hard men. Difficult men who have seen and done difficult things in difficult places. And for those reasons, maybe there is something about Amy's music that finds the soft places of us that somewhere remain within. She strikes a chord within us. And for a short time, for a few peaceful moments, there is nothing but the sweetness of her song and of who we were before. When we loved as she did and yearned for the warmth of affection and romance. When our hearts felt as if they might burst with all the love in them, all the want and all the ache.

Amy says the things that we wish we could and can no longer say. She says what we feel, and what we have all so desperately grasped for at one time or another. She embodies that thing that we have borne our battles for, that we have sought to stay alive for. Not for king or country or god or comrade, but maybe for the chance at going home and finding our own Amy. To have a life with and to protect. She touches a part of us that we are afraid of. Fearful of the delicacy of it. Of it slipping out from our fingertips. Of it falling away from us for good.

It is the part of us that makes *us* want to caress our partners and hug our children and pet our cats and talk in silly little voices to our dogs. It is the part of us that marvels at the big soft brown eyes of the cows grazing in the pasture we have stopped the car to get out and look at. It is the thing that the cows can sense, that we are not there to bother but to admire them, in all their gentleness and mouths chewing lazily on the brush behind the wire fencing. It is the thing that makes us take pictures with fascinated and silly boy smiles that our faces have not felt in too many decades.

What is it about men, she asks? But what is it about *us* men, I wonder? What is it about us former fighting men that makes us so afraid to bare this part of ourselves again? This part of us that wants so desperately for the cows to sniff our rough hands and allow us to pet their velvety noses. This part of us that looks forward to our serene morning car rides through the English countryside to our classroom in the Shropshire woods. This part of us that Amy somehow always finds when she so easily peels back the layers and memory of the armor that we have carried with us for too long.

It is the part of us that makes us save the candy from our rations to give to the children who run alongside our trucks and our tanks and our squads patrolling their markets and neighborhoods in our combat boots and our Kevlar and our rifles slung over shoulders. It is the part of us that still reaches down to comfort stray puppies and leaves out makeshift soda can bowls of water from our canteens. And it is the part of us that takes time out of our sleep schedules to write letters back to fifth grade schoolkids back home.

These are the parts of us which Amy finds her way to during our morning car rides to the classroom. Which, at times, have felt so far from us. Which we no longer quite allow free reign against the façade of our hypermasculine postwar selves. Which we now find ourselves afflicted by, an odd sense of guilt for allowing ourselves to feel such things again.

But why should we though? Feel any amount of guilt or shame for emotions of which any normal man would certainly have. Men who have not seen what we have. Are we not still just men who feel pain and remorse and love and want and deep sorrow? I think we are. I believe that this part of us that Amy finds is nearer to the surface than we would think. That it lies there dormant, still waiting and hopeful.

I will get an email while I am there from someone I once thought I loved, in what seems a long-ago past life. She will say that I am a drunk and cruel, and I will not say how this hurts me. I will say that she is weak and a coward and will not show her when I see her again how her words stung me. Or tell her about the time I was driving too fast in an African desert after thinking about such conversations for too long alone in a remote hotel bar–desperate to leave her behind–and came close to killing myself. Instead, I will mask my pain and show her the face I have worn in places of war, and she will see nothing there, only an expressionless void.

And I will retreat again into the comfortable circle of these other men who too often wear this same war face. I will tell them nothing about the email. And they will tell me nothing about the emails or phone calls from their own girlfriends or wives or partners that have also wounded them. Because that is not what men like us do. Instead, we trundle on in our warm little Toyota Prius wondering if someone else will ever touch that inner sanctum like Amy has, that hope of something more wonderful than breath and life.

I will not see these men for some time after this, or maybe ever again. We will go on to our various postings, some of us to Libya or Pakistan, others to Morocco or Yemen, and some back west. We will say our goodbyes in the way we do, with hearty backslaps and handshakes gripped for a moment longer than usual. We will tell each other to "keep your head down" and "your eyes peeled." We will light each other's cigarettes and give exaggerated salutes. This will be the way that we show our fondness for each other, our concern.

And what we will mostly take with us from this training in the Shropshire woods and listen to together in our offices and hotel rooms and tents and SUVs and buses and trains around the world will be Amy's music. And it will continue to touch that thing within us that nothing else can anymore.

The Suitors

A friend of mine killed himself some years back, put a bullet through his head after killing another man. I don't know how I feel about it yet. The last time I saw him alive we were celebrating being alive together at our company reunion. Alive from the war. Alive after his beating the latest bout of a life-threatening disease. And before that, I hadn't seen him since we had all returned home from Baghdad.

Since that evening, I have felt ashamed. Ashamed for having waited so long before being back in touch with him and for not having reached out during his hospitalizations. Actually, full disclosure: he was not really a good friend of mine. Well, that close of a friend. Or I was not as close or as good of a friend to him as I should have been. But we did survive Baghdad together, and that should have been enough. That should have meant something more than it did. I should have been there for him when he needed me. When he needed friends. When he needed a brother.

He had started talking to me about New York City after hearing me mention my working there in conversation with another friend of ours at the dinner table. We talked about me possibly visiting him one time at Mt. Sinai during his treatments. I should have gone. I should have reached out, asked if I could have helped him in some way. Even if it was just to keep him company for a couple hours, have a few laughs to take his mind off things.

I saw my friend again dead in his casket at the funeral home with our comrades in arms from his different deployments. He looked like I remembered him, thinner than he had been once, no hint of any trauma to his head, his face now forever stoic and still. I can't remember if he was in one of his dress uniforms or not, but I don't see why he wouldn't have been. It seems like something he would have wanted, and he had plenty of time to plan for such an occasion. But then again, I can't really claim to have known anything he would have wanted in the event of his untimely passing. I can't even claim to have really known much about him at all after our coming home, or him about me. What we knew about each other postwar, we mostly only knew from social media or from our platoonmates.

And I think it was like that for a lot of us. Those of us whose enlistments were up moved on with our lives. We went back to school and back to work, started families, traveled the world, moved out of state, lost track of each other. Others stayed in, reenlisted, transferred services, moved up the ranks, or deployed again to Iraq, as he had done. Some of us kept in closer touch with each other than others, some of us lost track of each other for a while before coming in contact again, and some of us we never heard from again. But my friend, he had kept in touch with a few of the same guys I still did, especially those he had deployed with a second time. And I would hear from them from time to time about him and others I had not heard from in a while.

No one from our company was killed in Iraq during the first go-round, or in their subsequent deployments to both there and Afghanistan, and for that we can count ourselves among the fortunate. But it was coming back home that was killing us. On motorcycles and in oncology wards, and hospices, in their own beds, and in backyards by their own hand, too many of us have taken their final breaths. Those who have died in motorcycle accidents, as I came close to doing myself once, I can make sense of. Risk taking behaviors, desires for freedom, the allure of the open road, the uncharted path, I get all of that too—I've been there. Cancers and other like causes of death, those I can comprehend as well. Taking one's own life intentionally, though—postwar—particularly after fighting so hard to remain amongst the living, is something else. Something for which there must be some other more complex reasoning.

"Why the fuck did he do it?" and "I don't know, man" and "So fucked up" were the common refrains. "He had just beat it again too," the cancer he had been struggling to shake for so long.

"I just don't know," someone would say quietly. "Those poor kids." And, "How could he?" And, "Motherfucker."

We curse him because of what he has done to himself, to his family, to the man he killed, and to that man's family. We curse him because of what he has done to us, because of what he has put on *us* now, the weightiness of his death, the stain of his blood on our consciences. Because he was one of ours. One of ours that we had somehow left behind, the cardinal sin of soldiers.

Why, brother? We all thought it then. And now. What could we have done, we wondered. And accused ourselves with it. Judged ourselves with it, with all the *what ifs*. What if I could have stopped it? What if I could have done something? We stay up alone at night with our glasses of whiskey and in our beds and on quiet streets in our patrol cars into the early hours of the mornings wondering if we could have stopped it, if we might have saved him. With a phone call, or a hospital visit, or something—anything within our power.

But could we have really, is the question. We have all felt the presence of the wolves circling at various times in our lives. Whether those wolves be in the form of a deadly illness or addiction, financial or marital woes, a crippling depression or anxiety or posttraumatic stress, an ex-boyfriend or former crush lurking in the shadows, or your fundamentalist Baptist in-laws praying for your death at home or abroad, they too often afflict us. Every now and again, we have fought them off only to have to later repel them again. Until we decide that we no longer have the will to, or possess the strength to, and one day just refuse to fight those wolves off. We bare our necks. We lay down our swords. When someone is intent on ending it, they are just going to end it. You are not supposed to say it, but it is the truth. Particularly with soldiers, fighters grown accustomed to being in it—the shit, that is—and pushing through and driving on, as we like to say. Soldiers are going to damn well do what they are going to do.

We have all felt the creeping unease and the trepidation of leaving those we care about behind. We wonder if they will wait for us. If they will be faithful to us. We hope they will be. But we never can really know. We try not to think about such things. But what if you are forced to think about these things because you have been given a literal death sentence upon coming home from one of your final stints in a warzone? What if you dodge the hangman once only to be given another death sentence right after escaping the last one? What if you have no other choice but to ruminate on these things because you know that you are not going to get out of it alive this time? What if the wolves are closing in, and all of these things are relentlessly spinning around your head, and you know you cannot fend off the wolves?

In *The Odyssey*, as Odysseus wanders, his wife Penelope and son await his return while the wolves encircle them in the form of a persistent barrage of suitors. In his long absence, these suitors envied him, and supped at his table, and drank his wine, and coveted his palace, and lusted after his wife, and lounged in his great halls waiting for her to finally give up Odysseus for dead in favor of one of them. Upon Odysseus's return, there is the inevitable slaughter of the suitors as they laze around drinking and feasting and hoping for his death, and one may have some difficulty feeling any sympathy for them as he exacts his vengeance upon them. Certainly, Odysseus did not.

I believe the wolves *were* closing in on my friend. I think they had been for a while, but this time he just didn't have it in him to keep the darkness at bay, these Odyssey suitors reincarnate, waiting for him to finally die. You don't survive two tours in Iraq and recurring cancer to one day just wake up and call it quits. There was something else there he could not escape.

Now he is gone, and I wish him peace.

SLOTH

The world breaks everyone and afterward many are strong at the broken places. But those that will not break it kills. It kills the very good and the very gentle and the very brave impartially. If you are none of these you can be sure it will kill you too but there will be no special hurry.

—Ernest Hemingway, *A Farewell to Arms*

Boanerges

T. E. Lawrence had seven motorbikes in the years after the First World War, all called Boanerges or Sons of Thunder. I had three, all called Black Velveteen after a Lenny Kravitz song. Beloved by us both, he died on his, and I came close to it on mine.

Motorcycles and combat veterans have always had a connection. Motorcycle clubs and motorcycles offer the veteran two vital things postwar: comradery and solitude, both of which the veteran needs in equal doses. From the brotherhood of former platoon mates, to the solitary veteran riding nowhere in particular, if just to lay waste to the noise in their mind, the connection is strong.

One morning, two summers ago, I woke up in an ambulance with a series of rapid-fire questions going through my head. How did I get here? Why are my arms and legs bandaged? What is this throbbing pain in my torso? I may have been saying these things aloud. Alone in the back of an ambulance, it's difficult to ascertain who's listening. At the very least, I knew I was alive and capable of conversation, and I knew my own name, too, which was reassuring.

When the ambulance slowed to a stop, the paramedics wheeled my gurney through sliding doors and into the building and I could see signs for "Poly-trauma," "Rehabilitation" and "Brain Injuries." Go figure.

I guess it was bound to happen. Like so many other veterans, after my return home I spent hours riding aimlessly past miles of woods and farmland and along the coast. The feeling of the sun on my face and wind in my hair and hearing the throaty rumble of torque propelling me fast and forward was soothing. I never imagined I might almost die on my motorcycle like two others from my company had since our return from Baghdad.

In my hospital room, a little TV hung from the ceiling, and I noticed a small bathroom off to the side. Monitors for vital signs and a small plastic pitcher of ice water on a tray sat nearby. My left arm was elevated by a little pulley system and a warm blanket was draped over me. I remember drifting off every now and then, waking up, and drifting off again. This was less because of the pain medication and more to do with the damage to my right frontal lobe, the part of the brain which manages things like personality and creativity.

Eventually, the attending physician approached my bedside. He told me that he was my neurologist, and that I'd been in a motorcycle accident. I was there because I'd sustained a traumatic brain injury.

I could believe the part about the accident. I felt like I'd been run over by a truck. But I could not recall a single second of it happening. Posttraumatic retrograde amnesia they call it.

It took a while to process. In all my years of riding on three continents, through busy cities, on bad roads and in all weather, I'd never had an accident. In the words of Paul Bäumer's character in *All Quiet on the Western Front*, "It is just as much a matter of chance that I am still alive as that I might have been hit." I guess my luck held. Lawrence's didn't. I can't imagine I even saw the car coming. All I know is that I lived.

Now, two years later and because of the police reports, I know that I was found "unconscious and did not present with an active airway." I know that my upper torso was "resting on the undercarriage of the motorcycle." From my family and doctors, I learned that I had broken ribs, a collapsed lung and ruptured spleen, among other injuries.

My beautiful Triumph Speedmaster that I'd devoted so many hours polishing and installing custom parts to make it louder, faster, and lovelier was equally mangled.

Luckily, the helmet I'd worn, and the police officer who responded that day, had saved my life.

After I was released, my friends would joke and ask if I'd seen Jesus or if I'd gone towards "the light." I don't remember seeing Jesus but of those long days and nights in hospital I do remember being wheeled around and moved from gurneys to beds with transfer boards. I remember feeling too tired to move or resist or stand up. I remember nurses waking me up telling me to swallow pills from little plastic cups and being injected in the stomach with an anticlotting medication. I remember the trays of food delivered twice a day and aides coming to change my bandages.

Since then, I've had a lot of time to think about reintegration, about veterans' adjustment back into postwar society, and why we find motorcycles, these mechanical beasts, so poignant.

A motorcycle is a live thing. A machine to be studied and learned from and listened to. It is no less intimate a relationship than the one between a soldier and their rifle. The soldier knows the rifle's intricacies and secrets. Likewise, the veteran knows the motorcycle's intricacies and fickle behaviors, its sounds, the difference between a content purr and an angry growl.

The relationship between man and machine is a relationship at which the veteran cannot fail. The veteran can be assured that their postwar persona will never disappoint a motorcycle.

T. E. Lawrence understood this. Shortly before his death on Boanerges, he wrote: "A skittish motorbike with a touch of blood in it is better than all the riding animals on Earth, because of its logical extension of our faculties, and the hint, the provocation, to excess conferred by its honeyed untiring smoothness."

I feel it, as much as other war vets. The motorcycle is better than all other means of transport on Earth, perhaps because it allows us to feel again.

The White Light

It is pretty easy to just lie there. To stare at white walls in an opiate haze and have people bring you your food and roll you over to sponge the chemical stink of hospital and near-death and despair off your skin. To just give it a rest for a bit, the struggling, the clamoring and grasping of one human speck amongst the horde. To give up on the wanting more, the earning, the positioning and politicking, the power struggling, and exertion of blood and sweat and intellectual capital. And when you do, and all that is there is you and the night and you alone with your thoughts, you will want nothing more but to lay there and let yourself be tired and be broken and not think about much anything else.

Katiana, the vocational rehabilitation counselor who would be eventually assigned to me, would call it apathy, a neurobehavioral disorder which can result from a brain injury and cause patients to have an absence of motivation, be prone to depression, and generally feel unemotional and uninterested. Apathy can inhibit overall recovery because the patient does not care if they recover anyway. The patient may believe they are never going to recover, becoming further depressed about their progress or current condition. It's not a condition one wants to have.

It's hard to say if I was apathetic or not. I don't remember much from those early weeks and months right after my accident. Having a moderate to severe brain injury is like living life in a blur or underwater. Everything is fuzzy. Your thoughts are like static between flipping channels on an old television set. Night turns to day, day to night, your circadian rhythm is off. Mine was flipped, and I would be wide awake at night and would sleep all day. And then sometimes I could not sleep at all at night—not with medication, not with meditation, not with lavender-scented spray, or structured breathing. Nothing worked.

Later, as I slowly progressed in my recovery and could get outside more and exercise more, sleep would become easier, and my day vs.

night sleeping schedule would slowly begin to even out. During that time, I would cycle on and off various sleeping medications as well trying to find the right one that wouldn't leave me feeling hungover for hours the following day. Soon my outpatient physical and cognitive therapies were progressing to the point where I was able to attend four days a week and my bones and burns and scabs were healing and causing me less and less pain.

But always questions plagued me, my trying to make sense of it, of my being there at the rehabilitation center. I had always emerged unscathed before. In all the places I had been, people I had crossed, wars I had stumbled my way through, minor injuries I had sustained, car accidents and rollovers and ramming of vehicles I had been involved in, I had always come out on top. "Tip-top," I would say. "No worries." Or, "It's all good." And then, and then this happened. My luck had just run out, I guess. My nine lives were up. No more ace up the sleeve for this unfortunate son.

Look at everything I had accomplished and escaped and survived, I would think. Look at me. Look at me and admire me for my greatness. Just a kid from the East Hartford projects, and I've been all over the world, to the ends of it, of civilization and humanity; and I've seen things, amazing things, and met amazing, exciting, and terrifying people. Look at me with all my skills and credentials, a half-breed, second-generation immigrant son from nothing and nowhere, a survivor and a fighter. I've dated elegant and classy ladies around the world. I have loved and lost and found and been beaten down and dragged myself back up by my bootstraps. Every single damned time.

And now this, the vengeance of the gods—or God or whomever I've too long defied. For my transgressions against them and theirs. A millimeter or so from being a vegetable is what they have rewarded me with. What is it then, this life they have granted me where I am little more than a prisoner? Of my shattered body and mind. Of my circumstances. Of the decisions I made, out of my loyalty to them and others so many years ago.

How will I beat this back, this fog of the mind, this near-constant exhaustion? How will I find my way back to who I was before this? Assertive leader of reconnaissance and security assessments in faraway lands inhabited by rogue militants and rebel forces, I once was. Am I still him? Still the analytical researcher of criminal organizations I used to be? The methodical student? The sensitive romantic? These are the uncertainties that kept me awake throughout the long days and even longer sleepless nights.

The world breaks everyone, Hemingway said—no matter how good, or gentle, or skilled, or credentialed, or brave you may be. And I believe it now. It will take me thirty-five years to believe it, but when I finally do, I will be struggling to keep my crayons within the lines of the cupcake coloring book page that I have chosen as my morning project. There was a time when I was making quick decisions affecting life or death, but not on this morning. On this morning, I will spend ten minutes debating whether to give my paper cupcakes orange or green or blue frosting. On this morning, this effort will consume all my faculties.

An hour later, after I have successfully shaded my cupcakes a delicious smattering of bright orange and woodland green, like confectionary hunters in a camouflage blind, I will commence learning—or relearning—to play the classic card game UNO with my classmates. I am told it is a classic card game anyway, but I cannot for the life of me remember ever playing it before. And so, we practice dealing the cards to each other and remembering the rules and playing hands of UNO before our supervised lunch.

"Whose turn is it?" the airline pilot who can no longer smell or taste or feel what food is hot or cold anymore is confused.

"Y . . . y-yours," the commercial real estate developer who was beaten and robbed and now has a permanent stutter says. And we continue our halfhearted, circular back-and-forth of green, blue, yellow, and red cards until someone says they have enough points to win or decides they are finished. I fucking hate playing UNO. I think we all do. UNO sucks.

We play until one of the staff members thankfully comes to take us to lunch at the cafeteria, and we make our way in a hobbling gypsy caravan down the hallway, a few of us still in casts and braces and in wheelchairs, some using canes or crutches. We are not permitted to eat on our own yet, because some of us need help eating, some of us do not know if we are eating, and some of us cannot taste what we are eating or know if we even want to. There is also the issue of ordering our food and carrying it, which some of us also need help doing. It takes about as much time to order and transport our food to the table as it does to eat it.

When we are finally sitting around the round lunch table, we are knights of a different order, a delicate order. One of broken knights at a round table of hemorrhagic strokes and intracranial aneurysms and frontal lobe hematomas and fractured bones and torn and burned and scarred skin and flesh and sinew and cartilage. We are former soldiers and bankers and airline pilots and real-estate agents and executives and once-skilled technicians and professionals who now must work together and use our combined remaining cognitive and physical capacities to open packets of mustard or mayonnaise to put on our premade plastic-wrapped turkey sandwiches. We talk about the same things over and over again, or nothing at all each day because no one remembers or cares what was said already or can think of anything new to say.

I tell the airline pilot to take it easy with the soup that he cannot taste or feel, because it is hot, and he is probably burning his mouth while our chaperone is helping one of the latecomers with their food tray.

"Why did he pick the soup if he can't taste it?" someone asks. "Aren't there easier things to eat?" The pilot shrugs. He says he felt like soup but forgot he can't taste it.

"That sucks," we say. It really does though. Of the few things we have left, poor guy can't even enjoy food.

The college student who fell off the back of her boyfriend's motorcycle doesn't want to eat anything except the ice cream, so we all pass ours over, which makes her happy. We are happy that she is happy. Her entire back had to be skin grafted after her accident. That sucks too. Skin injuries are the worst. At least mine were for me, the burns anyway. She doesn't remember much about it. None of us remember much. Posttraumatic retrograde amnesia, the doctors said. It's the brain's way of protecting us, apparently, our counselors tell us. Good old brain.

The guy who worked on movie sets is always hungry now, and

he eats a full hot lunch plate with all the sides and cake, followed by coffee and cookies later in the afternoon every day of the week. He doesn't remember if he was this hungry before. None of us think he could have been, him being kind of an average size and shape. He has to remember to ask his fiancé, he says. He better, we all agree, before he gets diabetes or something. He had just got engaged right before he had the stroke.

"Real shit luck, man." I say.

"Yeah, tell me about it. What about you?"

"Motorcycle. Right frontal lobe. Hit by two cars." He looks at me with the same look of dulled wonderment we all seem to have these days.

"Fuck, man. Real shit luck," he says. And we nod in solemn agreement and stare at our lunch trays overflowing in wrappers and plastic forks and knives and food remnants and soda bottles.

The chaperone helps everyone clean up the table and throw away the leftovers and walks us back to the classroom. Some of us split off to go to our individual physical therapies or other appointments and the rest of us fight to stay awake sipping coffee from Styrofoam cups.

"How is the sleep coming along? Did you try the melatonin? Did you practice your breathing? What about the meditation? Did you count while breathing? Five breaths in, five breaths out. . . ." Katiana fires off questions at us. She imitates the breathing, captivating us with her shiny lip gloss.

"Are you paying attention? What did I say? Okay, fill out two more job applications on the computer. Go," she orders me. I wondered once if she ever noticed any of us checking her out. If she did, she never let on. Or she was so used to the near continuous rotation of shattered men admiring her that she stopped paying it any mind. That or maybe she was just happy for us that we still felt anything at all.

At the end of our sessions she would bid me goodbye with "lots of white light and positive energy," and I would stare back at her blankly tilting my head like a German Shepherd puppy.

"The . . . what?"

"The white light," she explained. "It has healing powers. You can use it, even to help you sleep," she explained. "So, like, if I want to send white light to someone else, I can meditate in a quiet place, and think of them and give them the positive energy I've just created in that space. You should try it."

I looked at her dubiously. "Don't give me that look," she said. "Just try it. You have nothing to lose. And don't let me see you back here." And she laughed her perfect-toothed laugh and gave me a hug goodbye.

Send the white light. Send the white light, I find myself repeating silently sometimes at night or when I am all alone and it's quiet. I don't know where it is going or if it is going anywhere at all, but I send it out to her and other people who might need it from time to time. I hope she is doing the same somewhere, and the positive energy is still flowing. I think the white light and its healing powers must have worked its magic somehow seeing that I am still here and mostly recovered. I think it worked for me anyway. And probably for some of the others at the Knights of the Brain-Damaged Round Lunch Table.

I have felt it when I don't want to get out of bed in the morning or the afternoon or the evening or whenever I finally awake. Every time there is another refusal or rejection or setback, Katiana's white light is there. When my heart has been broken and mended and rebroken and re-mended, and it seems like there is nothing and no one else to look forward to, then I believe—I want to believe—that somewhere out there, the white light is waiting to enfold me in its protection and energy and push me back up on my feet again. And if I ever go to back to the deserts, out into the darkness of the wilderness soul-searching again, then I hope Katiana's white light is out there illuminating my path.

It has to be. I think it will be; because if Katiana believes in it, then I don't see any reason why I shouldn't believe in it either. In some ways I think the white light has always been there, and each of us are custodians of that light—wherever we, and it, may be—and it is up to us to pass on that light to whoever we see that needs it, like she did for me. I never saw the "Jesus light" when I was unconscious in the trauma ward like my friends would later ask me, but I did learn about the white light from Katiana. Maybe if there was more white light to go around, the world wouldn't be such a messed-up place. And if there were more Katianas in the world spreading the white light around, we would all be better humans because of it.

A Special Form Of Incoherence

You wonder what I am doing? Well, so do I, in truth. Days seem to
dawn, suns to shine, evenings to follow, and then I sleep. What I have
done, what I am doing, what I am going to do, puzzle and bewilder
me. Have you ever been a leaf and fallen from your tree in autumn
and been really puzzled about it? That's the feeling.

−T. E. Lawrence, letter to Eric Kennington, May 6, 1935

"**P**seudopsychopathic syndrome," which can develop as a result
of traumatic brain injury and damage to the frontal lobes, is a
condition characterized by "sham rage-like reactions, emotional and
social instability, aggressive behavior (at times), cognitive disturbances
described as a special form of incoherence, abnormal social behavior
in the form of social adhesiveness, carelessness and a certain proneness
to criminality. All of these phenomena are stressed by alcohol even in
small amounts."

While working on the railroad one September afternoon in
1848, a foreman by the name of Phineas Gage was supervising the
blasting of rock near Cavendish, Vermont. One minute, he was doing
what bosses do, and the next, he—or someone near him—sparked a
gunpowder-filled drill hole and blasted a tamping iron through the
left side of his face. The tamping iron, at just over thirteen pounds
and three-and-a-half feet long, skewered his head, piercing below his
left cheekbone and behind his left eye, passing through his brain's left
frontal lobe and exiting at the top of his skull. Legend has it that ole
Phineas, being the tough New England bastard that he was, walked
away from the site of the accident like a human shish kebab and found
his way to a doctor under his own steam. He was even awake as the
doctor extracted the offending iron from his head.

With the exception of a few minor complications, like a fungal
infection and the eventual loss of his left eye which would stay sewn

shut for the duration of his life, Phineas Gage is said to have gone on to live a relatively exciting-sounding and, for the most part, full—albeit short-lived—remainder of his thirty-six years. After traveling around showing off his tamping iron along with the remnants of the hole in his head for a fee, at what one might imagine were kids' parties and other fun gigs, he would go on to take up a residency at a museum in New York, follow the gold rush to Chile, and drive horse coaches, eventually making his way to California and dying of seizures while working on a farm.

From the sound of it, via the limited and varying records and accounts that there are, Phineas made the best of an incredibly bad situation. He also, according to reports by doctors who had evaluated him, changed in some ways and not for the better. Once considered to be thoughtful and courteous, a gentleman and businessman both, he now was described as unhinged, promiscuous, foulmouthed, and prone to drinking and brawling. Other descriptions and daguerreotype images picture a vastly different Phineas. Indeed, this Phineas appears more as a dignified and still dashing pirate, his left eye closed and his tamping iron brandished tight in front of him.

We will never know which Phineas Gage was the real Phineas Gage, or the most like himself prior to his having an iron spike javelined through the head, but having some damage to my own frontal lobe—in my case, the right side—I can imagine some of what his life may have been like for him post-impalement. What is remarkable in both of our cases, nonetheless, is that first, we both lived through and with grievous injury. And second, that we somehow managed not to kill ourselves after. In regard to Phineas Gage, I have to admit, I am more than impressed with the guy's determination and sheer grit. I surely could not have done it while being down an eye, *and* suffering from a brain injury, *and* making a life in a foreign country where I didn't speak the language. By some means, I guess he came to the conclusion that he was just not done living yet, regardless of the circumstance.

I can only imagine what life must have been like for him, continuedly fatigued and foggy, irritated about something he couldn't quite remember, depressed and anxious and needing a drink or five, just to dull the trepidation of going out in public. What did they think of him with his peculiar look and even more peculiar new personality? What did he think of them? Were they cruel to him? Did they make fun of his missing eye or his mannerisms or the divot in his skull? Did they think him weird or odd or deformed or less of a man? What did they say to him? Imagine what a day in the life of Phineas Gage after his injury might have sounded like:

"Hey, heads up, it's Phineas." Or "Hey, Phineas, you heading this way?" Or "Whatcha looking at, Phineas?"

"Oh, there's Phineas again, stumbling around drunk. What a mess, that lowlife."

"Hey Captain Ahab, you catching any whales today?"

"Brain's all turned to mush on that guy."

"Keep him away from your womenfolk. I hear he's a downright savage."

"Yeah, that's when he can stand upright on his own."

"That poor son of a bitch. He's about as good as a gourd. No good to the railroad anymore."

"Did you pay the dime to put a finger in the hole in his head? Whatever's left of his brain is still pulsing in there."

"Yeah?"

"Oh, I shit you not, good sir. Took the wife and kids to the museum for a laugh. A real walking science project this fella."

"I hear he's gone pretty much insane now, huh?"

"Oh, definitely. Guy's a freak. Just hangs out in bars gargling back whiskey and balancing shot glasses in the hole in his head and picking up the local whores."

"No way."

"Oh, yes, my friend, señoritas and all. Word is he's got himself a little Chilean honey back there too."

"Dastardly deeds that, I tell ya."

"For sure. Keep an eye on your wife. Ladies buy that sorry, sad sappiness. He'll ravage her yet if ya let him. And you'll never get her back."

People are cruel. Phineas's brain and personality and emotional responses had been restructured—fractured even. If indeed he acted in the ways he did, brawling and drinking and going from the gentleman he once was to the opposite end of the spectrum, who are we really to judge? And, the question remains as to whether or not this new persona, entirely true or not as the reports have been distorted over the centuries, and the pseudo-psychopathic syndrome rage-like reactions that he exhibited were a result of his altered brain or an inherent response to how he perceived he was being treated by those around him. I am no physician, clearly, but I have been both a human being and a brain patient. And I have to say that I am all the way in the Phineas corner on this one. If his behavior was even partially motivated by his ill-treatment by his fellow man, it was probably justified.

Was it a persona he could control, this raging, whoring, drunken fool, as sometimes he was described? One he affected or invented to somehow push back at and survive the society he felt he was no longer a part of that now looked at him like a walking science project? Or was he nothing like this character he played at all and still very much the person he had always been but had just not found his place again? I like to think he was still very much himself somewhere within, and that eventually he did find his place, maybe in Chile where he had run off to. Perhaps finding some peace and comfort in the solitude of driving those horse coaches and love with some dusky Chilean maiden.

The society he no longer felt a part of then is not dissimilar to the one that so many veterans of war have difficulties returning to today, many having also suffered horrific injuries both to the brain and elsewhere. The struggle to find one's place again after sustaining such wounds, physical and mental, too often results in a special form of incoherence both for the veteran and society around him. They no longer understand or recognize it, nor does it understand or recognize them. When Phineas left for Chile, it is less likely that he left in search of striking it rich in the rush for gold than it is he was running away from the discomfort and disconnect he felt at home after his accident.

Veterans of war and brain injury survivors, some of us who fall into both of those categories, feel this incoherence more than most. We feel the separation that this incoherence causes, for us, for those we love, and for those we would like to know and to understand us once more. There is some Phineas in all of us who have survived the traumas of war and horrific life-changing, personality-altering injuries to our bodies and our souls. We too may have had a cocktail or a glass of wine too many and stumbled into the wrong person at the wrong time, or over ourselves when we least wanted or needed to. We too have felt the bewilderment and anger and anxiety and depression that comes with adjusting to our new civilian lives and altered personas. We too have reacted on a hair-trigger of excessive anger and "sham rage" at perceived slights or insult for reasons we cannot quite comprehend.

A slip of the hand, a tipped and broken glass, an angry bartender, some heated words exchanged, and I am Phineas getting tossed from a dive bar in Hell's Kitchen, barstool and all. Or stumbling through a university reading with nerves steeled by whiskey and pills and falling over myself on the way out the door amidst concerned faculty and friends. Or repeating the same sentence in the same story while my dinner companions look at me in utter bewilderment as if my brain is glitching and my vocabulary is on a limited loop like an electric train doing laps under a Christmas tree.

Long before I was like Phineas, and just another veteran of a too-long war trying to find his place again in life, I too left for a faraway place. My sojourn in Sudan was my own pursuit of what I imagine he was also searching for in Chile, in his own faraway place, for something that had eluded him in his own country. Peace maybe. Belonging. A new sense of purpose. Or the solitude that was never a possibility at home given his grisly new celebrity. Some or all of these things may have been an equal draw to the former railroad man turned museum curiosity. A need to escape that way of life perhaps. Had enough of the stares and scrutiny. The snide comments. The whispers and pointing. If only to salvage the dignity he had left.

And I can sympathize with him. My leaving an easy life in the Connecticut suburbs for the desert climate and hardship of Darfur was not a difficult choice for me. I was not visually changed or scarred like Phineas. But I still had to get away. And what I found there that I had not yet found back at home, was a peace that came with the solitude of my being there. Wilfred Thesiger, an Oxford-educated former soldier who spent decades living in among the Bedouin tribes, talks about this feeling in his book *Arabian Sands*: "The Empty Quarter offered me the chance to win distinction as a traveler; but I believed that it could give me more than this, that in those empty wastes I could find the peace that comes with solitude, and, among the Bedu, comradeship in a hostile world."

And maybe Phineas also found this peace that came with the solitude of his being at the front of a horse coach in Chile picking up and dropping off passengers at their various destinations—far away from the land of his birth and anyone who had ever known him prior to or post-brain injury.

Maybe on one of those long, solitary journeys, Phineas—quiet and polite and still dapper as he is, even if just for a simple livery driver—picks up some lovely farmgirl on her way to the market, and she strikes up a conversation in her limited English. She is curious and smiles and has long dark hair in braids and rosy cheeks and a red nose from the morning cold and asks about his left eye that is sewn shut and the droopy hat that he wears with the brim pulled low as if to try and conceal that part of his face. She makes a motion like a knife stabbing and asks him if he is a pirate, teasing, and smiling at him. And Phineas picks her up the next morning and the morning after that. She invites him over for dinner with her family, and he shows her his scars one quiet evening, and she weeps for him and smooths his hair over the divot in his skull. And Phineas loves the farmgirl from Chile, and she loves him, and they get married in an apple orchard with dancing and their families and friends.

It could have happened that way. I hope it did, both for Phineas and for the romantic still somewhere within me, under all that fog and static and carelessness and incoherence that has bested me on too many occasions. Blaise Pascal, French physicist and philosopher, wrote in his posthumously published collection of thoughts, *Pensées*, "Le coeur a ses raisons que le raison ne connaît point," a message that translates to "the heart has its reasons that reason does not know." Pascal, being the scholar that he was, observed correctly that the heart, at times, supersedes the brain. And I think it has for myself and Phineas Gage, and likely old Thesiger too, as we all went to faraway places in search of something else—something the heart deemed necessary—something the heart demanded regardless of any other interference of brain or mind or reasoning.

The Long March

In the brisk of the early morning in late autumn, with just a hint of frost coating the blades of grass and the first rays of sun just beginning to brighten the sky, the soldier slept. Curled up on a wooden bench, his jacket pulled tight around his neck, his boots and gaiters still on and fastened around his ankles and calves, he slept soundly with fingers hooked into the leather shoulder strap leading to the worn, brown-leather Sam Browne belt around his waist.

"Hey there. Hey. Hey, wake up there. Are you okay?" The officer tried first talking to the soldier and then shaking him lightly by the shoulder.

"Huh? Whaa?" The soldier awoke with a start and rubbed his eyes as if he had woken up from a long-needed rest after an all-night patrol or a sleepless night staring off into no man's land waiting for the Huns to appear.

"I said, 'are you okay? Do you know where you are?' "

"Uhh. No, sir, I'm not exactly sure, sir." The solder shook his head and looked up at the officer with a confused look on his face.

"Do you have your driver's license on you?"

"Yes, sir." The soldier sat up and pulled out a wallet and handed the police officer his license.

The soldier was not actually a soldier. Well, he was once but was not anymore. Not that long ago. Well, kind of long ago, but not 100-years-ago long ago. Anyway, that soldier was me. I was that "soldier." I explained the situation and, miraculously, the officer offered to drive me to the town line at the edge of his jurisdiction, which I gratefully excepted. He was an older guy, wearing one of the old leather patrol jackets. And he had a sense of humor, another thing I could count in my favor.

"I guess ya never seen that before, huh?" I said to the police officer who laughed and shook his head no.

"Love the uniform though," he said. "I wish I could take you further,

173

but just keep walking that way. You'll run straight into Montclair."

We shook hands, and I thanked the officer for being a fine American before saluting smartly and stepping off with a click of my boot heels onto the leafy sidewalks of Verona, New Jersey. At about 6:00 a.m., the fall air was still brisk and just a small glimmer of sun was starting to warm my face as I marched towards home in a full 1917 US military World War I Doughboy uniform, one that I had pieced together off Etsy and eBay.

Admittedly, morning walks in such attire these days are not the norm for most people, and neither are they for me, as exhilarating as they might sound. Though, the thick wool did keep me warm on that cold October morning, and I did quite like it and grew rather fond of its ancient, hidden-away-in-a-closet-like smell.

As one of a pair of Gatsby era costume wearers for a Halloween party, I did my best to reprise Robert Redford's Gatsby in the original cinematic role while Juliana went as a society gal, feather boa, fishnets, sequins, and all. It really did have the makings of a fabulous evening, at first. And then, inevitably, we drank too much. Then we argued about something. And then we drank some more, and argued some more, and at some point, I decided that I was just going to walk home. So, I started walking. Or running. I may have run for a bit too to blow off some steam. But that was a couple towns over and a few miles away from mine.

Your left right. Right-ooooo left. Your lefffffffffft right, righto left. Left righto left, left righto left, your left right, righto left. I kept the cadence and time in my head as I passed newspaper delivery boys and early risers walking their dogs and looking at me with their heads cocked to the side in wonderment.

As I kept my step, I thought about the thousands of men who marched and died in this same uniform so many years ago at the Somme and the Marne and Belleau Wood and the Argonne Forest on so many colder mornings, and I made myself forget about being cold and tired and hungover. I thought about Juliana and where she thought I was, and if she had called because my phone's battery was dead. I thought that I would like to be home where it was warm, and where I could make myself a nice hot cup of coffee and apologize for being such an asshole. I wondered what we were even arguing about. I wondered if I should just keep marching until I ran out of road to march on. I wondered if the rust-colored stains on my jacket were dried blood from a hundred years ago.

I wondered if the men and boys from Verona marched down these sidewalks once, never to return or maybe to return different men from the ones that left–boys no longer boys, young men no longer young. I wondered if they lugged their heavy duffel bags and rucksacks to buses crammed with other young men and boys, their warm breath hanging in the cool morning air like mine, and their coarse woolen uniform blouses and sweaters scratching their necks like mine. I wondered if these same trees shed the same color leaves those young men and boys tread on in their boots over these same sidewalks and if those young men and boys walked past some of these same houses– the old Dutch Colonials and classic Georgians and Tudors sprinkling the still green landscapes of the quiet neighborhoods and neat rows of homes and yards they once played and worked in.

What were they thinking as they walked away from their lives, these men and boys from New Jersey who, some of whom, would end up fighting and dying in the muddy trenches and fields of France and Belgium so far from where they were born and raised across the sea? How many of them had done so? How many survived to return and live long and productive and happy lives back here in West Orange and Verona and Montclair? How many would return and become police officers like I once had been? How many would be teachers or professors? How many would dress up as soldiers from wars fought centuries ago for Halloween parties and stagger out into the dark after arguing with their girlfriends or partners or wives? These are the things one wonders when they are marching alone in the early morning hours.

I put one foot in front of the other as I have on many other mindless treks through wood and field and town without putting much thought into it. The repetitive nature and low cognitive exertion required for marching is good for thinking, I decided. Walking is good for recovering brain patients, I thought. I definitely heard that somewhere, probably at my cognitive rehabilitation, and I wondered why I hadn't taken long walks more often. I decide then that I must have gotten lazy somehow. Or preoccupied with things that are less important than they really are. At one time in my life I did like taking long walks, I remembered. And I'd explore towns and cities around the world on foot for hours on end. Those were the good old days maybe. When life was simpler, maybe. When I too was a soldier and still young and strong like other young soldiers.

But then I thought again about soldiers dying. That the soldier who wore the uniform I was wearing then, whose dried blood was still on it, might have died in it; him never having the chance to just take a walk across town kicking up orange and red and brown leaves out of his way without a care in the world. And then I felt sad for him and all the soldiers who died in that war. And for soldiers in all wars. Though, maybe the soldier whose uniform I was wearing didn't die. Maybe he had a traumatic brain injury from a mortar shell exploding too close to his position and was safely evacuated to a field hospital. And because I could, because I had the luxury of doing so, I decided that my uniform's soldier lived. I gave our uniform a good ending, a more uplifting ending. In my borrowed uniform's story, its soldier comes home despite his brain injury and lives a good long life as a schoolteacher. Or a farmer. Or something that made him happy and didn't stress him out too much.

And as I marched, step after step, mile after mile, closer to Montclair, making up stories about the soldier of the uniform I was wearing—closer to the apartment and the woman inside that apartment who I was sure would be pissed—I couldn't stop thinking about all those dead and wounded Doughboys and all those dead and wounded Tommies, envying their not having to face their pissed-off wives or partners. But then I remembered the mortars and the terror and the rats and the screams of the dying men across the trenches that they had to face instead, and I am ashamed of my ever thinking this. I said a quick prayer for the souls of those dead and wounded Doughboys and Tommies and ask for forgiveness from the God I have too often ignored.

I thought about Juliana and me. It wasn't so bad, for the most part. When it was bad, it was really bad, for sure, but when it was good, it was really good too. There was actually a time when we liked each other—when we were in love even—when spoke to each other without arguing, and I didn't decide to walk home inebriated in a full World War I infantry uniform. I don't remember when that was exactly, or when it ended, but I'm sure there had been a time like that. When we were kids basically. Teenagers. Before there were babies and jobs and mortgages and bills to pay and mouths to feed. Before there were wars to go to and children to lose touch with and humanitarian crises to run away to and find one's self halfway across the world. Before there were corporate salaries, and mutual temptations and betrayals and hurt and loathing, it had been a pretty nice life.

We just lost each other somehow, somewhere along the way. Wanted different things. She wanted the house and the white picket fence, and I wanted to go to school and see the world. Both equally worthy endeavors I can say now that I'm almost twenty years older and have lived a little more. We did do both of those things at various times eventually. It just got away from us in the end. And maybe people just aren't meant to be together their whole lives. Who really ever knows though? Fuck all if I do. At least we tried harder than most. Morning marches make sense of everything.

Forty-five minutes passed as I plodded on. In the distance, at the end of the treelined, neatly cut front lawns and seasonally decorated front porches and doors, I could see the outline of the furniture store on the intersection of Bloomfield and Fullerton Avenues in downtown Montclair. Soon I saw the library and the Congregational church and the Unitarian church and the Episcopal church with their Love All—Serve All, Hard Rock Café-like mantras posted everywhere and wished one of them was open so I could use its restroom. And then I remembered the Starbucks where the homeless people tended to gather, and I praised the Trinity for Seattle-brewed commercialized coffee. Lucky break, I thought. And I'll fit right in.

Airborne Rangerrrrr, life of dangerrrrr. Airborne Ranger, Airborne Ranger how did you gooooo? Oh, yes, I was stoked now about the prospect of taking a nice, long piss and acquiring a bottle of water and a steaming hot Americano looming on the horizon. Damn, Sarge, I congratulated myself. I still sing a great cadence, even if I am singing it to myself—in my head. Silently. While walking down Church Street in full World War I regalia. *In a C-130 flying lowwwww. And when I get to heavennnnn, old Saint Peter's going to sayyyyayyyyy. I made my living as an Airborne Rangerrrrr, life of danger!* Which I didn't at all since I was an MP, but that's the marching cadence everyone sang in basic training and the one that stuck.

"Oh hey, man. Nice getup," the bearded, flannelled barista said to me when I ordered. "Long night?" I told him he had no idea and not to ask, and he laughed. I'm sure he saw the remnants of many a long night and long walks of shame on many a weekend morning in Montclair. Definitely none involving a World War I-era US Army Model 1917 Service wool tunic, tapered laced leg breeches, brown leather boots and gaiters topped off with a Sam Browne belt and cross shoulder strap smelling of stale whiskey and vodka shots worn by someone looking like he spent the night curled up outside of a senior citizens' home though. He handed me my Americano for which I was unabashedly grateful, and so I tipped him five dollars. I wasn't going to need it where was I'm going anyway, I thought—which was straight to hell when Juliana runs me over with her Subaru.

A homeless man stared at me as if he wasn't sure if he was still coming down from whatever crystal meth high he was on and was seeing crazy things, and I gave him a nod as if to say: "Yes, sir, whatever it is you think you're seeing here right now in this moment, you really are. And good day to you, sir." Of course, I didn't actually say that. Because *that* would be, well, just too weird. Not to mention rude. And I'm sure the homeless in Montclair are not treated with the utmost respect, it being a rather well-to-do kind of place fixated on its veneer. I bowed slightly and left for the final leg of my journey home feeling almost human again with my coffee and my water.

Without a working phone or my keys in my possession, I rang the buzzer to the apartment and waited. When the door opened, it was exactly like I envisioned. Juliana was pissed and had been obviously crying with the remnants of her flapper-era makeup still on and her mascara still smeared. "Where . . . the . . . fuck . . . were . . . you?" she said in a low, measured voice.

"Well . . .," I say, not entirely unapologetically. "I walked."

"No, fucking shit! I called the police and filed a missing persons report. I thought you were going to get hit by a car or walk off a bridge or something." Her voice grew higher by the second.

"You did what?" I laughed but not because anything was funny anymore—a nervous laugh, a worried laugh. I collapsed on the couch with my coffee to untie my boots and give the dog, who was excitedly wagging his tail and sniffing my ancient-wool-clad legs, a pat. At least he was happy to see me.

"I didn't know what the fuck you were going to do. I told the police you were wandering around with a brain injury in a World War I uniform."

"Oh, awesome," I deadpanned. "That's just great. Did they believe you? What the hell did they say?"

"They said they'd keep an eye out for you. It was too early for a missing person case. You hadn't been gone long enough. I have to call them back."

When the police arrived, she let them in, and they walked over to where I was still sitting on the couch with my Americano, petting our dog in my World War I 1917 US Army-issued, olive drab wool Expeditionary Force uniform. *Oh, yeah, take this all in fellas. This is a once-in-a-lifetime viewing. You'll never see this again.*

"Sir? How are you feeling? Is everything okay?"

"I'm good," I said. "Everything is grrrrreat."

They asked me a few more questions, of the health and welfare type, and one of the officers talked to Juliana while the other took me outside the apartment doorway to talk to me in private.

"You sure you're good, man? I was a Marine. You know there was some talk about you . . . maybe . . . ," the officer hesitated.

"Killing myself?" I interject. "Yeah, I'm not going to off myself—not intentionally. I don't have PTSD. I'm not senile or anything. She was just upset. I'm fine now. I just had too much to drink, and I decided to walk it off. I fell asleep on the way home."

"Happens to the best of us. You take care of yourself now."

I heard him on his radio with the dispatcher as they were leaving, "Oh, yeah . . . she wasn't kidding. Full friggin' World War I uniform. Drank too much. Oh, yeah, yep, seems okay. Clear it."

I went back to sitting on the couch with the dog while Juliana continued to yell at me for my stupidity and selfishness and the overall messed up state of things between us and everything our life had become. I agreed with her. I, too, wondered how the hell we ended up this way. How I ended up this way. How I went from one day sitting down with armed militias and rebel groups to negotiate passage for the NGO I worked for, to stumbling drunk from West Orange to Montclair dressed like a doughboy ready for a bayonet charge in the Marne.

And what happened to us? To our being in love once. To our little family. What was it that got in the way of us? The war. The separations. The reconciliations. What chain of events has caused this travesty of whatever this was now? How did we get to this point? Where neither of us are even sure of what we want. I wondered why we were still doing this—if we even loved each other anymore. Or if maybe we still did on some strange level. Somewhere, somehow, we've both strayed or stayed and found our way back to each other.

"I think we need help. I need help. Maybe we both need help," I said. Or she said it. Maybe we both did. Hopefully one day, we'll figure things out.

Marriages are long marches in their own right. Sometimes they plod along one foot in front of the other like a well-oiled machine. Other times, they are not so smooth, and they are confusing and uphill or assailed from all sides. My own, a product of the war I went to, has not been easy, as many a marriage conceived by wartime obligations often is not. Many of the marriages of the men and women I went to war with did not survive their homecomings and the adjustment to life afterward. I wondered how many of those doughboys' and Tommies' marriages didn't make it either way back then. I wondered if the soldier whose uniform I had slept in had a marriage that lasted. It is a difficult thing for the wife or husband or partner who is left behind in wartime while their other half is away at war. And I cannot blame Juliana for the difficulties we have had together postwar. That blame lies with me.

Epistle To A Commander

Do you remember sitting cross-legged in the sand near the wadi, Commander? What did you do, and where did you go after I last saw you?

Oh, there's something I wanted to ask you still. Was it on your orders that my trucks were taken at gunpoint? You know how afraid that made my people when it happened, I'm sure. What did you think might happen—that I wouldn't somehow find out it was you regardless of whether it was my trucks or another NGO's? And how did you end up punishing those boys who took them when you discovered those trucks were mine? But why would you punish them anyway for carrying out your commands? Anyway—I hope they are well, *inshallah*. And that they grew up to be better men than us.

How many battles did you fight after I left you, Commander? And did you live to ride again on your fast camel or in the Toyota and feel the wind in your hair and the sand clinging to your skin and sticking to your uniform?

Ah, yes, the sand, Commander. We talked about this too. It's the stuff that gets stuck in the bolts and magazines and jams the mechanisms of your rifles.

Do you think of me, Commander, as I think of you from time to time? Do you ever wonder where I am and what I am doing now? I think about you too. I wonder if you have married again as you said you might and, if you have more children who weigh as heavily on your mind as you go into battle.

I wonder if you fight for or against the government now or for other governments even. If now you are in Yemen, Commander—in a land very far from your own.

Are the desert winds the same? Are the clouds of dust as dark and the sandstorms as forceful? Does the rain fall in dirty, heavy drops laden with the fine desert dust that blows through the air and stains your clothes as it mixes with the blood of those whom you have slain? Do the winds of war blot out all life and moisture and breath and thought and flesh and air too, as it felt like to those of us who have been there?

Do you still carry my lensatic compass, Commander, that I carried through my own war? Remember that I promised you that it was a good talisman? It was for me, and I pray it has been for you as well.

I hope you are still with us, Commander. I hope you will grow old enough to see your children and grandchildren grow up too. *Inshallah.*

Well, Commander, I will give you a summary of what it is I am doing now since it has been too long since our last meeting. I am no longer who I was then, a young man, with the fearlessness of the young. Now, my hair and beard have more gray in them than I would like and you would remember. As I imagine yours has now too.

My bones ache when I wake in the morning now. And it takes more and more very dark and strong coffee to shake the sleep from my brain.

Speaking of my brain, I was in a motorcycle accident a few years ago. Remember we spoke of my motorcycle? I showed you pictures of it. Made in England. "Inggg-glannd," you said. We practiced saying it. You and a few of your young fighters as we smoked my Lucky Strikes under the tall tree. That was a good day, we had together, Commander. I remember it fondly.

Ah, yes, the accident. I broke quite a few bones. I hit my head pretty hard. Right frontal lobe hematoma they call it. A bruise on your brain. I awoke a few days later in hospital. My motorcycle was destroyed, unfortunately. And I don't ride anymore, no.

Because this is for the more daring. I am not the same as I was when I met you, as I mentioned. I am no longer running as I was in those days. Running from the cries of the stagnant toward the beckoning taste of the whirlwind. The whirlwind is a young man's seductress as you know, Commander. As I know now. And to ride it to the end of its path is too often a tragedy.

Commander, the things I thought of to tell you as I lay there in hospital mending my bruised skull and brain and shattered bones and flesh. I cannot recall them all—I still struggle to remember some things.

You know, I thought about going back to the army in my country for a time after I left you. Or the French Foreign Legion if they would take me. Do you know the Legion, Commander? Anyway, I did not. I finished at the university I had mentioned to you and worked for the police again for some years—but the restlessness still swirled within. You know that feeling? The restlessness? I know you do, Commander. It's been some time since I've talked to someone like you.

Oh, I wanted to talk to you about something else now. I am a teacher now, in New York City. Only a couple days a week, as I will be returning to university again myself for doctoral studies. But I wanted to do something worthy of this second life I've been given. Even if it's just a few students whom I might steer in the right direction or propel to something greater, maybe that is just as well and as good as anything else I could possibly do, I'd think?

What would you do, Commander, if you could leave this all behind you—lean your rifles to rest against the willows and beat your swords into plowshares, as they say? Would you return to your fields of sorghum and millet and groundnut and watch as your sons and daughters climb the date palms and hide amongst the sheep and goat herds as they graze? Would you play dominoes as your wives attend to their stews and their breads as we once did so long ago? Would you wake to the sounds of the roosters crowing and the donkeys braying in the early morning hours for the prayer? *Alhamdulillah*, Commander. I hope that you would.

So, the thing I've been wondering—if you are in Yemen or elsewhere? Chad or Eritrea or Ethiopia even—I hope you can find the strength to defend those weaker than you. And by this, I mean those who come from where you came from—where we came from—and who are only trying to make a better life for themselves and their own children. You know what I am saying, Commander. You have a choice to make. Not only with those who don't carry the rifle but with your own young men.

I think many of them are with you not because they exactly want to be, but more so because they have no other great opportunities. Ah, and this is the heart of it—the thing I've been wanting to talk about with you that I have been trying to remember. We are not who we are because we wanted to be this way, do you agree? We became fighters because this was our lot. And not because it was the thing that was our preference.

Commander, I have heard from the international news of the

young men of Darfur being recruited into service to fight for the Saudi princes and being killed by the dozen. That these young men are barely in their teenage years, whose families have very little to subsist on. Young men of the Jebel Marra and Umm Al-Qura and Um Gunya and Marla who have survived their own government's oppressive forces only to go and die for another's.

Yes, you know these young men, Commander. You were them once. And they were you. They are your sons and your brothers. You are their father and their uncle. So, if you are indeed there with them, you have an obligation to bring them home—you know this, right? Have not you been through enough, you sons of the 'Fur?

There is a story in my country of an army major, Dick Winters, who when fighting in the Second World War, promised himself that if he lived through the war he "would find a small farm somewhere in the Pennsylvania countryside and spend the remainder of his life in quiet and peace." I often think of Major Winters's promise and the promises that I also made to myself in my own war in Baghdad. I promised myself that I, too, would live a quiet life—one by the sea.

I've not yet fulfilled all of those promises I made, Commander. But I am trying. It's why I left you. I had to suppress that soldier who still lives within me. Though he is fading as I grow older, and with my age, so does the youthful urge to take such risks as I have.

Commander, I would like to see the little daughter I showed you, in the photo that I kept in my wallet, grow up. I would like to grow old by the sea with the woman I love, and play with my daughter's children the silly games which all grandparents play with their grandchildren, that make them laugh and clap their little fat hands.

You know these games, Commander. I smiled as you bounced your small son on your knees during our meetings so long ago. I hope he is well and grown tall and strong. I also hope he has not become a fighter as we once were.

Godspeed then, Commander. May Allah bless you to live to grow old by the wadis near which you and I walked hand in hand, as is your custom. May you tend your own small farm and your orange trees and enjoy many plentiful harvests for many more years. May you never again fire a rifle in anger, brother. Pray for me as I will pray for you.

Afterword

Morning comes. I go to my class. There sit the little ones with folded arms. In their eyes is still all the shy astonishment of the childish years. They look up at me so trustingly, so believingly—and suddenly I get a spasm over the heart...Here I stand and must now be your teacher and guide. What should I teach you? . . . Should I tell you that all learning, all culture, all science is nothing but hideous mockery, so long as mankind makes war in the name of God and humanity with gas, iron, explosive and fire? What should I teach you then, you little creatures who alone have remained unspotted by the terrible years?

—Erich Maria Remarque, The Road Back

I teach now too, college in New York City. And when I teach, I sometimes wonder what to say, what to teach, like Ernst, in *The Road Back*. They look at me in the same way, my students, hanging on my words, as if they are of some deep meaningful origin—which of course, they are not. The innocence they possess, it frightens me. And what is it that I should teach them now, after coming home from my war? Should I tell them how to run convoys through hostile cities, how best to ram through a roadblock. Shall I teach them how to duck down in the gun turret at night so as not to get clotheslined and lynched by low-hanging power lines? Shall I teach them how to keep the sand out of their ammunition magazines and their firing bolts lubricated so their weapons do not misfire? Should I demonstrate the methods of room clearing with various rifles, pistols, and shotguns? Should I march them to the edge of exhaustion in the afternoon heat?

Or should I tell them of the helplessness as the light fades from a man's eyes and his blood seeps through his uniform and runs down his shattered limbs? Or to hold the door open for a man's departing soul as his medics rush his failing body through on a stretcher? Should

I tell them of the sudden terror they will feel when they see a plastic bag in the roadway, or a dead dog, or possum, or deer and the potential ordnance their hollowed-out body cavities may now contain? What of the traffic coming to a halt on one's way to work? Am I to warn them of the panic they will feel as they cannot maneuver their car around it, as they instinctively search the corners and shadows and windows and rooftops for phantom gunmen they will know are not really there? What of the anxiety they will feel in the crowds of train stations and subways and pedestrians walking close, pressed against the masses of so many unknown strangers?

Am I to tell them of the coming home angry and drunk and going to bed angry and drunk and ignoring the cries of girlfriends and wives and lovers and partners and waking up an empty, shadow of the person you once were? Am I to tell them of lovers lost and of the heartbreak and disappointment of years and thousands of miles and lives apart, of once-entwined hearts unraveled and souls grown distant? Am I to tell them of the guilt and sadness of leaving small children they may never know? Or of young love grown brittle and old too soon, and too easily fractured once returned from the foreign fields and jungles and sandy swaths? Am I to tell them of the sorrow they will feel of losing friends to those foreign fields and of the guilt they will have after continuing to lose those friends long after they have all returned?

What of the depths of depression they might find themselves spiraling downwards in, in bars and pubs and with their bottles of whiskey and vodka and prescription pills and photos of lost lovers and partners and friends and family? Am I to tell them of the cold they will feel in the lonely hours late at night while they are sleeping restlessly on the floor with the dog, wrapped in an old poncho liner? Or of the chill of the hard-plastic seating in the back of police patrol cars and of drafty local lockups and glazed icy stares of homeless vagrants? Or of prolonged solitary walks in frigid winter air after missing their train stops long after the taxis are on the roads and their families have gone to sleep without hearing from them or knowing where they might be? Or of the pity-filled expressions of emergency room doctors and nurses after hearing who they were once and seeing what they are now?

I cannot. I do not wish it for them, not any of these things. And I will not tell them of the vain glories of crisp uniforms and smart salutes and shiny bits of metal pinned to one's chest. I will not tell them of those lessons too hard learned and too easily forgotten. Of the unraveling of one's soul. These lessons I cannot teach them, nor must I. These lessons are only for we who have borne the battle, who volunteered in place of our fellow citizens, in place of them.

When they do ask me things about war, about the army, I usually answer in mundanities. So as not to make it sound too interesting maybe. Or to not give them any ideas. Inevitably, some of them will enlist. They will use me as a reference for their background investigations, or I will write them letters of recommendation. And when they do enlist, I hope they will get posted someplace boring and safe. Like Nebraska. Or Wyoming. And I realize that I am getting old. Old enough to worry about things like this. Old enough to admit that I love them, these kids, as much as they irritate the hell out of me with their excuses and their tardiness and their refusal to read their assigned chapters. Old enough to halfheartedly consider going with them in case anything happens. As if my rickety middle-aged body could handle it or if the military would let me back in without a binder full of waivers.

It was over twenty years ago that I first went through Army Basic Combat Training at eighteen years old, full of teenage angst, a chip on my shoulder, and an insatiable need to escape my life and see more of the world than small-town Connecticut. And how I have changed since then. How the world has changed. I am not the same person I was when I first enlisted, or when I deployed to and returned from Baghdad, or after having gone to and come back from Darfur, and who I am now. I am still adjusting from the experiences of having been in those places, my roles in each, whether my presence contributed for good or ill, and the memories of who and what I've left in those places and in between. The road back for me is still unfolding, and my struggle at times to find my footing, has not been without regret. My sins, likewise, have not been without their toll on me and on those I care about. This I know.

So, what should I teach them then? Maybe I will teach them what

I now believe real courage is and isn't. Real courage is not marching ten abreast toward unarmed civilians with riot batons and shields and tear gas at your disposal. Real courage is not arresting children because of the color of their skin or the authority of your badge. Real courage is White Helmets digging through rubble in Syria. Real courage is facing down the most powerful men in the world and testifying about your sexual assault. Real courage is defending the weak and giving a voice to the voiceless. Real courage is refusing to give up and give in when everything within you is telling you that you cannot go on. Real courage is risking your own life so that others may live. Real courage is not squandering that life.

And that might be the best thing I could ever teach them.

References

Code of Federal Regulations (CFR), Title 38, Chapter I–Department of Veterans Affairs §4.130 Schedule of ratings–Mental disorders.

WRATH
Waller, Willard. *The Veteran Comes Back*. London: Forgotten Books Classic Reprint Series, 2012.

LUST
Remarque, Erich Maria. *The Road Back*. Boston: Ballantine Publishing Group, 1931, 191.

"A 9/11 Story"
US Army Field Manual, No. 3-22.68, Crew-Served Machine Guns, 5.56-mm AND 7.62-mm. Washington, DC: Department of the Army, 2003.

GLUTTONY
Homer, *The Odyssey*.
Homer. *The Odyssey: The Fitzgerald Translation*. United States: Farrar, Straus and Giroux, 1998, 176.
Lawrence, T. E. *The Mint*.
Lawrence, T. E. *The Mint: Lawrence After Arabia*. United Kingdom: Bloomsbury USA, 2016, 206.

HUBRIS
Knowles, Elizabeth, ed. *The Oxford Dictionary of Phrase and Fable*. Oxford: Oxford University Press, 2006, 341.

A Special Form Of Incoherence
Peters, Uwe H. "The pseudopsychopathic personality and the limbic system." *Neuroscience & Biobehavioral Review*, Autumn 1983;7(3):409-11. doi: 10.1016/0149-7634(83)90046-5.

Twomey, Steve. "Phineas Gage: Neuroscience's Most Famous Patient." *Smithsonian Magazine*, January 2010.

SLOTH

"Epistle to a Commander"
Winters, Dick, and Cole C. Kingseed. *Beyond Band of Brothers: The War Memoirs of Major Dick Winters*. Toronto: Dutton Caliber, 2006.

AFTERWORD
Remarque, Erich Maria. *The Road Back*. Boston: Ballantine Publishing Group, 1931, 231-232.

Acknowledgments

"We Who Walk Among You" and "The Desert" were originally published in *Military Experience and the Arts*.

"Allawi" appeared originally in *War, Literature & the Arts*.

"The Fat Sergeant Major" appears in different form in *The Wrath Bearing Tree* as "The Hideous Hypocrisy of Himmelstoss."

"In Defiance of the Gods" appeared originally in *Litro Magazine*.

"This Cruel Land" appeared originally in The Waterston Desert Writing Prize's Anthology *Deserts*.

"Praying" appeared originally in different form in *The Globe and Mail* as "Ibrahim, my driver and my guide."

"Boanerges" appeared originally in different form in *The Globe and Mail* as "Road Warrior."

The Monadnock Essay Collection Prize

This contest was started in 2017 to encourage essayists to gather their work into book form. The prize is awarded for a book-length collection (120-160 pages or 50,000-60,000 words) of nonfiction essays. The essays can take any form: personal essays, memoir in essay form, narrative nonfiction, commentary, travel, historical account etc.

For more guidelines please go to our web page or to Submittable:
www.bauhanpublishing.com/the-monadnock-essay-collection-prize/
or to www.bauhanpublishing.submittable.com/submit

NEIL MATHISON was winner of the first **Monadnock Essay Collection Prize**, in 2016. In 2017 his collection *Volcano, an A to Z* was published. He is an essayist and short story writer who lives in Seattle, Washington, Friday Harbor, Washington, and Ketchum, Idaho.

KIRSTI SANDY was winner of the second Monadnock Essay Collection Prize, in 2017. In 2018 her collection *She Lived, and the Other Girls Died* was published. Sandy teaches creative nonfiction, memoir, and narrative theory at Keene State College.

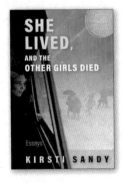

Michael William Palmer was the winner of the third Monadnock Essay Collection Prize in 2018. *Baptizing the Dead and Other Jobs* tells a coming of age story set in the heart of Mormon Country: Utah County, Utah.